Chinese Learning Journeys:
Chasing the Dream

Edited by Feng Su

Trentham Books

Stoke on Trent, UK and Sterling, USA

Trentham Books Limited
Westview House   22883 Quicksilver Drive
734 London Road   Sterling
Oakhill   VA 20166-2012
Stoke on Trent   USA
Staffordshire
England ST4 5NP

First published 2011

British Library Cataloguing-in-Publication Data
A catalogue record for this book is available from the British Library

ISBN: 978 1 85856 477 7

Photo credit: *Many thanks to Liverpool Hope University's Marketing
Department for permission to use the copyright protected images
for the cover.*

Designed and typeset by Trentham Books Ltd
Printed and bound in Great Britain by 4edge Limited, Hockley.

For Caroline and Ella, with love

The life stories recounted in Feng Su's book are epic journeys into the unknown. This inspiring volume shows the tenacity of these outstanding individuals, as they dig deep into their reserves of cultural and linguistic courage to pursue their dreams in the face of daunting challenges. – **Professor Bob Adamson, Hong Kong Institute of Education, Hong Kong**

This is a fascinating collection of narratives telling us of a widely varying range of personal 'learning journeys'. It is an important reminder that the academy must provide a context or a 'habitat' that can nurture a wide range of learning journeys and a new diversity of educational dreams. – **Professor Jerry Wellington, University of Sheffield, UK**

Our bookshelves groan under the weight of explanations for the juggernaut of globalisation and China's multidimensional entanglement with it. This modest book, with more heart than pages, lightens the load a bit through first-person accounts of eight Chinese sojourners chasing their dreams across a diaspora of learning and living. Reflecting the universal human condition that life's transformative lessons are unpredictable and always unfinished, these intimate accounts of wrenching homesickness, indomitable will to achieve, and sheer delight in the wonder of the world are interwoven with epochal changes that have moved China from famine in the late 1950s to the glaring disparities of 2010's post-socialism. Central to each story is the development of what Catherine Bateson has called peripheral vision, a rooted yet empathetic ability to scan one's horizon for life-enabling serendipity. While these tales of persistence, hard work, and self doubt and cultivation are quintessentially Chinese, travellers of all origins will recognise in each story the leap of faith that translates confusion, persistence, and hard-won knowledge into hope, humanity, and future. Yes, 'everything can disappear overnight,' formal schooling is not always a pretty affair, foreign languages befuddle the tongue and numb the mind, and doctoral training can feel like a battle fought on three continents. But along the way education can help us know ourselves and others; can cultivate the dispositions of patience, careful listening, and humility necessary for appreciating difference; can mobilise resilience and resoluteness of purpose in the face of setback. Jon Nixon captures these lessons in a proverb-inspired epilogue worthy of each seeker's frailties and courage: 'the wind got up in the night and took our plans away'. Feng Su has produced a little gem of a book that quietly celebrates the choices we are capable of making when hard winds blow. – **Professor Heidi Ross at Indiana University, USA**

Feng Su's study provides a fascinating insight into the learning journeys of Chinese students. We follow richly diverse narratives of schooldays in China, the huge challenges of studying in English in British universities, the making of new friends, and the taking of community jobs, all of which transform the learner and engage the reader. – **Associate Professor Anne Hickling-Hudson at Queensland University of Technology, Australia**

Contents

Foreword

Since this is a narrative volume, or more precisely a volume of the narratives of Chinese learners reflecting upon their experiences in a wider world, I will begin this foreword with a small piece of my own narrative. When Mao Zedong died in the summer of 1976, followed shortly by the arrest of his closest collaborators, the so-called 'Gang of Four,' I was a young Canadian teacher in Hong Kong. I had been observing China from this vantage point since 1967, but had been unable to get a visa to visit. When Deng Xiaoping came forward at this important juncture to declare that China would now open up to 'modernisation, the world and the future,' I caught a vision that has stayed with me ever since. Education would be the first priority in this opening up, and education would transform China from an isolated and inward turned society to a dynamic outreaching society, that would be in a position to share its rich cultural heritage and civilisation with the world. I committed myself to contributing to this process of transformation, first through teaching in Shanghai in the early 1980s and secondly through researching both the internal and external consequences of the opening up. It has been quite a journey!

It thus gives me great pleasure to say a few words about the stories of Chinese learners collected in this fascinating volume. With typical modesty many of them have focused on unique aspects of their experiences of learning and professional development in England and elsewhere, and said less about the contributions they have made and are making. Almost all of the authors have begun their narratives from early childhood, depicting difficult and impoverished environments in rural China and the ways in which the sudden opening up of the educational system gave them the opportunity to 'chase their dreams'. All are part of the huge number of Chinese students and scholars who have found their way to different learning environments around the world and often stayed to make unique professional contributions. As of 2009, the tally of Chinese students going abroad since 1978 is 1.62 million, with 497,000 having returned to China. With the acceleration of reform and openness the annual return rate has risen dramatically in recent years, from 10,000 in 2000 to about 42,000 in 2006, 69,300 in 2008, and 108,300 in 2009 (Pan, 2011).

The other piece of this story relates to the nature of the contribution being made by those million plus Chinese learners who have opted not to return for the time being at least. This book gives us fascinating insights into the professional career developments of some of these people, and the ways in which they are enriching the increasingly diverse environments of universities and other professional organisations in England and Wales, Hong Kong and elsewhere. Many have stayed in contact with colleagues and family members in China and some are making extraordinary efforts to contribute from afar to the remarkable transformations coming about in Chinese education and society. In this sense they are a part of the other side of the story of openness in China's recent development – the fact that China has become the sixth destination of choice for students from around the world, after the USA, the UK, Germany, France and Australia, with over 200,000 international students enrolled in Chinese universities in 2009 (CSC, 2009), up from 10,000 in 1991, 52,000 in 2000, 85,000 in 2002, 141,087 in 2005 and 195,503 in 2007 (Hayhoe and Liu, 2010).

This volume contributes in significant ways to a rich and growing literature on the Chinese learner complementing other recent titles such as *Revisiting the Chinese Learner: changing contexts, changing Education* (Chan and Rao, 2009) and *International Education and the Chinese Learner* (Ryan and Sleuthaug, 2010).

Ruth Hayhoe
Professor, Ontario Institute for Studies in Education,
University of Toronto
President emerita, The Hong Kong Institute of Education

Editorial preface

This book charts the learning journeys undertaken by eight Chinese learners across national and continental boundaries and socio-cultural contexts. All eight contributors are originally from mainland China and each chapter takes the form of a reflective autobiographical account of their experiences of studying both in China and overseas. Their reflections are structured around the turning points and life changing choices they have had to make in chasing their dreams.

The book has its origins in my doctoral study of the Chinese international student experience of UK higher education: *Transformations through Learning* (Su, 2010). Although the analysis I developed in that study informs the focus of this book, I feel it is important that the contributions speak for themselves without any prior editorial interpretation. All I would want to say by way of guidance to the reader is that the narrative form – the idea of the learning journey as a passage across time and space – is a central feature of each of the chapters and reflects my own concern as editor with learning as both holistic and multi-layered. The significance lies in the story.

Other than that I simply want to express two hopes for this book. I hope, first, that it will contribute to our understanding of the Chinese learner's overseas experience and how that experience is shaping the aspirations of a future generation of Chinese citizens. Their dreams of the future will shape not only their own individual fates, but also the future of Chinese society. It is this generation – informed by international travel and overseas study – that will play a leading role in the creation of the emergent China.

Second, I hope that the book will contribute to our understanding of what it means to be a learner in the 21st Century regardless of our particular origins and destinations. All the contributions to this volume relate in their different ways to the complex and turbulent history of China over the last fifty years. However, the major themes of border-crossing and inter-connectivity impinge on us all. In a world shaped by forces of globalisation, the experience of transition and displacement is one we all share.

Acknowledgements

Many people have helped me while I was editing this book. In particular, I thank Jon Nixon for his generosity in sharing his thoughts on many aspects of the writing and, more importantly, for the warmth of his friendship. I owe special thanks to Bob Adamson for his detailed and thoughtful comments on an early draft of this book. Thanks also to Pauline Nixon for her final read-through. I thank my publisher, Gillian Klein, for having trust in me and providing advice and encouragement which I desperately needed during the process of editing this book. Thanks also to Liverpool Hope University for grants which enabled me to attend conferences to meet with the contributors of various chapters. I thank Bart McGettrick and Wendy Bignold, at the Faculty of Education of Liverpool Hope University, for their support. Finally, I thank my family who have always been there for me. Without their love and support, I could not possibly have completed this book.

Feng Su
November 2010

A note on terminology

There are two approaches to presenting Chinese names in English. One is to follow the Chinese convention and present the family name followed by the given name. An alternative approach is to follow the Anglo-American convention in presenting the given name followed by the family name. The second approach has been adopted in this book, since some contributors have previously used this form in their published work and most use it routinely for their professional work.

The term 'China' used in this book refers to The People's Republic of China (PRC), which governs mainland China and two special administrative regions – Hong Kong and Macau. It should not be confused with The Republic of China (ROC), which is the 'official' name for Taiwan.

Notes on contributors

Anwei Feng, PhD, is a Reader in Education and Director of the Graduate School in the College of Education and Lifelong Learning (CELL) at Bangor University, UK. He has had teaching and research experience in tertiary institutions in a number of countries including China, Qatar, Hong Kong, Singapore as well as the UK. His recent publications include *English Language across Greater China* (2011); *Becoming Interculturally Competent through Education and Training* (2009, with M. Byram and M. Fleming) and *Bilingual Education in China: practices, policies and concepts* (2007), all published by Multilingual Matters.

Xiang Li, BA, is a Graduate Trainee in an oil corporation in Hong Kong. She has studied in Sun Yat-Sen University in China and Liverpool Hope University in the UK. She has a combined degree in Linguistics and Business Studies. Her research interest is in the area of second language acquisition. In her spare time, she enjoys playing basketball, listening to BBC radio and volunteering for charities.

Jue Jun Lu, LLM, is a solicitor at an international law firm in London. She completed her secondary education in Shanghai, China. During her seven years in the UK, she has studied and worked in Chester, Liverpool and London. She speaks Mandarin, Shanghainese, Cantonese and Spanish. She holds a first class law degree, a Distinction in vocational legal training (Legal Practice Course) and an LLM in Professional Legal Practice. Her interests include swimming, karate, trekking and travelling.

Jon Nixon, PhD, has held chairs at four UK universities and currently holds an honorary chair at the University of Sheffield, UK. His publications include, *Interpretive Pedagogies for Higher Education: Arendt, Berger, Said, Nussbaum and their legacies* (Continuum, 2011), *Higher Education and the Public Good: imagining the university* (Continuum, 2010), *Towards the Virtuous University: the moral bases of academic practice* (Routledge, 2008), and (edited with B. Adamson and F. Su) *The Reorientation of Higher Education: compliance and defiance* (Springer and CERC of The University of Hong Kong, 2011).

Feng Su, PhD, is a Research Fellow at Liverpool Hope University, UK. He has studied and worked in China and the UK. His primary research interest is in cross-cultural learning contexts and the development of the learner within higher education settings with particular reference to overseas students. He is the co-editor (with B. Adamson and J. Nixon) of *The Reorientation of Higher Education: compliance and defiance*. He is currently working (with B. McGettrick) on an edited book *Professional Ethics: education for a humane society*.

Mamtimyn Sunuodula, MA, is a specialist in Asian and Middle Eastern languages and information resources at Durham University, UK. He studied and lectured in educational psychology in China before coming to the UK. He was a lecturer in psychology and conducted research on Uyghur education in Xinjiang. He has worked for the BBC World Service and the British Library. He currently teaches research skills to postgraduate students and conducts research in the field of second language learning and identity.

Wenli Wu, PhD, is a Post Doctoral Researcher in a university in Hong Kong. She gained her doctoral degree from the University of Warwick, UK. Her doctoral research explores international East Asian postgraduate students' experience of cross-cultural adjustment in UK higher education. During her seven years' study in the UK, she worked as a Chinese language tutor, international officer and interpreter at the same university. Previously, she was a qualified English language teacher in China. Her current research interest lies in second language acquisition.

Jesse Chiu Lai Yi, MA, is a teacher of Japanese Language in Hong Kong. She has studied and worked in Hong Kong, Japan, UK and Korea. She speaks fluent Cantonese, Mandarin, Japanese, English and Korean. She holds a combined degree in Business and Multimedia technology awarded by University of Liverpool, UK and a MA degree in Japanese Language and Teaching awarded by the Chinese University of Hong Kong.

Xiaowei Zhou, PhD, has recently completed her doctoral study at the University of Manchester, UK. She also has a BA in English Language and Literature and an MA in Linguistics from Peking University, China. Her doctoral research explores the narrativised academic experiences of six Chinese students studying an Economics related master programme in the UK with a focus on the phenomenon of academic acculturation, the complexities of culture and the culturality of individuals.

1

A Chinese lecturer in an English university: an unfinished journey

Feng Su

I was born in 1978. The province in which my hometown is located is mainly agriculture based. My parents were working in a small factory at the time – my father was a technician and my mother was a factory worker on the production line. My grandparents were living in a small village near the town. One year later, my younger brother was born. Due to the start of one of the most controversial social policies of all time (Greenhalgh, 2008) – the one-child policy in China in 1979 – my parents were penalised for having two boys. Their salaries were frozen for a year, which made life extremely hard for the family. We barely survived. Among my earliest recollections, the most memorable moment was my birthday each year because my mum would give me a boiled egg as a birthday present. My dream at the time was to be able to have a proper birthday celebration although I did not know what would have counted as a proper one. Since then, I have not been keen on celebrating birthdays. They remind me of the tough living conditions in the past.

School years in the Chinese countryside

I started primary school at the age of 8. There were no kindergartens or nurseries available in the town. Even if they had been available, my family probably would not have been able to afford them. There were five compulsory years of primary school education at that time – now there are six. When I was in the second year, my parents left the factory and started their own small manufacturing business. In 1988, it was still rare to see private businesses in inland China as the government had, until very recently, viewed them as a form of evil capitalism. The factory employed about ten workers. It was very challenging for my parents to make a profit because there was not much support for private business in the form of credit from banks and networks for selling the products across regions. They were too busy with the business to look after two young boys at home. As a result, they decided to send the older one – me – to stay with a distant relative in a remote village named Xuezhuan about fifteen kilometres from my home town.

Being a child, I was not very happy to leave home to study in the remote countryside. It meant that I had to leave my friends, family and familiar environment, and venture into the unknown. The living conditions and harshness of the life in the village were much worse than I had expected. There was no electricity and the nearest town was five kilometres away; drinking water was taken from a community well. It took about 30 minutes to walk to the village primary school in a field, and when it rained or snowed, it took much longer. However, the family I stayed with treated me like one of their own and I started to get to know some of the neighbours' children. In the following two years, I was fully engaged with life in the village. Like many other children, I had to work in the fields after school, particularly in harvest seasons. I remember looking after a horse, two cattle and a number of sheep.

School life was not as challenging as in my home town. The main subjects included Chinese literature, Mathematics, History and Physical Education-my favourite subject because I would get the opportunity to play in the fields next to the school. English was not yet offered as a subject. I did not start learning English until a few years later when I went to a city high school. However, in primary schools in China today, many students are learning English from year three. At present, English is compulsory throughout primary and secondary schooling, and in higher education, and is learned even in kindergartens in some coastal cities. In retrospect, government attitudes and policies towards English have been shaped by China's relationship with the outside world and by the political, social and economical development of China. Historically English, as a foreign language, can be regarded as a barometer of modernisation (Ross, 1992). My father's generation would have taken Russian as a compulsory school subject in the 1950s given China's close relationship with the former Soviet Union.

There was some fun living in the countryside. For instance, there was no big pressure to excel at school as long as you could pass the class tests. I would treasure all the opportunities for entertainment, like going to a movie, even if this meant walking miles to another village in the evening. This was often a treat for me and other kids because it only happened on special occasions like weddings and the birth of baby boys. The movies were shown in an open field with the help of a petrol-powered electricity generator. While you were enjoying the movie, you would pray for good weather so it would not be interrupted. The love of movies stays with me today. The conditions for watching movies have improved beyond my wildest imagination, from an open field to a 3D IMAX cinema in the UK many years later.

My mother visited me from time to time, but I rarely went home due to the distance. It was both the happiest and the saddest time when my mother visited me; it was very sad to say goodbye to her at the end of each visit. I did not like village life most of the time and I found it difficult. I always dreamt of leaving the village and being reunited with my family in the town. However, those two years provided me with an opportunity to witness how harsh life could be in rural China. Many years later, whenever I have a difficult time, I always tell myself there could not be anything worse than coping with life in that village. If you really dislike or fear such conditions, you will work harder to make a difference. Now I believe my experiences in those two years have motivated me to strive against the odds in my later life. Every time I recollect life in the village, I feel appreciative even though I did not see it that way at the time.

Becoming a Communist in China

After a two-year stay in the countryside, I was reunited with my family. Not long afterwards, we moved to a small city and my parents gave up their private business and joined a state-owned factory as engineers. The main reason for the move was that my father wanted my brother and me to get a better education.

Along with the one-child policy, there is an equally infamous and controversial family registration policy in China. The *hukou* is a household registration record and a residence permit which identifies a Chinese person as a resident of one area and holds personal information on all members in the family, such as name, date of birth, name of parents and name of spouse if married. There are two kinds of *hukou*, one for rural residents and one for city dwellers. It has been used by the authorities to control the flow of residents from rural areas to cities. The *hukou* makes a huge difference to a Chinese person's life. An urban *hukou* brings with it a number of benefits, such as education, employment, housing and health care which are not available to a rural *hukou* holder. If a person wants to live in a city, permission has to be obtained from the authorities. It has effectively and unfairly created two tiers of social class, based on where a person is born. In recent years, the *hukou* system has been relaxed a little, due to the mass migration of workers from rural areas to cities to seek a better life and drive the growth of the Chinese economy. However, in the 1980s it was very difficult to change the *hukou* from one category to another. My parents did so by giving up their small private business in exchange for the right to move to a small city and work in a state-run factory. Only children of urban *hukou* holders could attend city schools.

The high school years in the city were a struggle for me. I attributed this to the fact that I had received a disadvantaged primary school education in the small town and the countryside. I sometimes even found it difficult to make myself understood because of my strong regional accent. I had to learn standard Mandarin Chinese along with a number of challenging subjects. English was the most difficult subject for me and I did not enjoy it. English classes focused on grammar rules and vocabulary. There was little speaking practice. I could not see the point of studying it apart from the fact that it was a compulsory subject for the National College Entrance Exam (NCEE). At the time, I longed for the day when I would no longer have to learn English. Ironically, many years later English became my second language and I use it daily.

Confucius says: 'to be fond of something is better than merely to know it, and to find joy in it is better than merely to be fond of it' (Confucius, *The Analects*, Book VI, 20). This is a true reflection on my experience of learning. I did not find much enjoyment in studying during high school years because it felt like every lesson taught was exam preparation. I tried my best and made a real effort to catch up with the rest of the class. However, I did not do very well in the NCEE in 1996. I only managed to be accepted on a two-year diploma course in a provincial agricultural university. I was admitted to study Food Sanitation and Quarantine, which was not the course of my choice.

To my surprise, I enjoyed every minute of the two years at the agricultural university. It was located in Zhengzhou, a provincial city famous for its light industry and for serving as a transportation hub linking many parts of China. Studying at the university provided me with a new perspective on life. If the experience of living in a village showed me how harsh life could be in China, then my initial university experience convinced me how wonderful life and the future could be in a metropolitan city. Without the burden of exams, I enjoyed learning more and participating fully in the many activities organised by university student societies and associations. Each term I was rewarded with a small scholarship based on my academic performance; I was an athlete competing in the 10,000 metre races and I was even selected to join the Communist Party at the end of the first university year. Joining the Communist Party was not a result of my political beliefs. Instead, it was a recognition and reward for my personal achievements in university life.

Everything seemed very rosy and, like many other university students, I was expecting to be assigned a job by the state after my graduation. However, in 1998, the job assignment policy was abolished by the central government in the context of the decentralisation of state-owned enterprises and cutting the number of civil servants. It was difficult to find a job in Zhengzhou and I returned home. There were no jobs for graduates in my home city. Both my parents had left the state-owned factory and had set up a new private business to support the family. My younger brother was helping them. I did not want to be involved in the business as I did not wish to stay in the same city after I had seen the outside world.

In 1998, I left home and went to the capital city, Beijing, to take another two-year diploma course in Business English at China Agricultural University. In the context of opening up Chinese markets to foreign companies, the ability to speak good English was considered desirable for a decent job in Beijing. Under pressure to make a living, English became the centre of my academic life in those two years. I had not enjoyed studying English as a school subject because of its focus on grammar. To develop an interest in the language, I started to listen to English-language radio stations like the BBC and Voice of America. I was helped by the fact that there were a number of American language tutors who taught us English speaking skills. To practise my spoken English, I was one of the eager students in the class who liked to answer tutors' questions. Gradually I developed confidence in speaking English. As a by-product of learning English with American tutors, I now speak English with a trace of a North American accent.

In July 2000, I finished my studies with reasonable English proficiency and started to look for a job in Beijing. It was challenging but, after a number of attempts, I found a job as a Marketing Manager Assistant in a medium-sized computer software company in Zhongguanchun in Beijing – China's Silicon Valley. The company specialises in developing and producing software applications for the Globe Positioning System (GPS) and electronic maps. It was exciting to work in the information technology (IT) industry as it was predicted that IT would transform people's lives and the way of conducting business. The job involved travelling around China to attend IT exhibitions including some international ones. My English skills were put into practice in the workplace when foreign business partners visited the company.

Two years later, it seemed that I had reached a glass ceiling in my career. There were no prospects of promotion as I needed higher academic qualifications and experience of working in a different company. I did not see any possibility of advancing my career without these credentials. I was planning to move to another job in an internet company after a headhunting agent approached me. However, this did not work out, after the internet bubble in China burst in 2002. With small savings and family support, I decided to study in the UK to pursue a master's degree.

Learning to study in the UK

By studying in the UK, I have benefited from different approaches to learning and interactions with British people. As a result, I have had the opportunity to reflect on the difference between Chinese and English approaches to learning in a university setting; my experience of interacting with local people has also enabled me to think about the differences between a western democratic society and an authoritarian Chinese one.

Before I came to the UK, my impression of Britain came mainly from classic novels like *Jane Eyre, Pride and Prejudice, Oliver Twist*, and *A Tale of Two Cities*. I had read these books when I studied English in Beijing. I imagined that it would always be raining in the UK and people would always take an umbrella with them when they went out; everyone would act politely and dress formally like a gentleman or a lady. Obviously, my image of Britain was romanticised by my reading of English literature. Some of my images of England turned out to be true while many others were far from reality.

In 2003, I arrived in the UK for the first time and started with an intensive English course prior to the planned master's degree at one of the universities in Liverpool. On my arrival, I felt a mixture of excitement and anxiety. It was wonderful to be able to see blue skies (on dry days) and vast green spaces around the campus. It was a huge contrast to Beijing's often murky skies, which many believe are a result of the pollution by heavy industries around the city and busy traffic inside it. However, Liverpool seemed much quieter and smaller compared to Beijing.

After a number of years studying English in China, it was a shock to discover how little I could understand local people and make myself understood when I arrived in Britain. There were strange accents, fast speech, and unfamiliar phrases and slang. Even after my first three months, I was still struggling with English language proficiency. I then realised that it was not possible for me to improve my language skills dramatically and develop a deep understanding of British culture within one year. Subsequently, I changed my study plan to a three-year undergraduate degree in Information Technology.

The way of teaching in a university in the UK is very different from China. Perhaps under the influence of Confucian traditions, teaching in

Chinese universities is teacher-centred and takes place in large classes. The focus is on formal lectures, with little interaction between students and academics. In contrast, UK universities tend to encourage inter-action and discussion between tutors and students, which helps foster independent thinking. For instance, I had a Computer Network Security module that was entirely delivered through the problem-based learning (PBL) approach, which encouraged students to solve given problems on their own. The tutors were facilitators rather than know-ledge transmitters. This different teaching method encouraged me to become an independent learner and to be critical in the learning of new knowledge.

The only difficulty I had was becoming part of the learning community on campus. In Chinese universities, all students are required to live on campus and stay in a dormitory. It is common to see six or more stu-dents sharing one room, and I once shared a room with seven other students when I studied in Beijing. It is easy to feel part of a community, a very intimate one in terms of getting to know each other. Many of my life-long friends and enemies came from these student dormitories.

When I arrived in the UK, I was allocated individual student accommo-dation on campus. At the beginning, it was such a luxury to have my own en-suite individual room and nobody interfering with my privacy. Gradually, this became a barrier between me and other students as everyone seemed to stay in their own room. I had few opportunities to meet them, let alone develop some sort of friendship. There was a strong sense of loneliness. I had to learn to cope with the fact that my family and friends were on the other side of the planet, and I could not afford to telephone them all the time. My only comfort was to meet with fellow Chinese students on campus who were sharing a similar ex-perience. I met my future partner, Caroline, in this way.

With my knowledge from working in the IT industry I did pretty well in the degree. I was awarded first class honours. However, during those three years, I had to work extremely hard to support myself financially. My part-time work ranged from being a bar cleaner, restaurant waiter, chef, university library assistant, community volunteer, IT technician to university teaching assistant. Now, looking back, I believe these part-time jobs were a very important part of my overseas study experience.

They provided not only financial benefits but also learning opportunities to improve my English, and to get to know British people and the local culture from a different perspective outside the university.

When doing voluntary work with a local computer centre, UK Online, I met some local people who were receiving benefits from the state including housing benefit, child benefit and unemployment benefit. I learned for the first time that, as well as the free National Health Service (NHS), people who are unemployed or in disadvantaged circumstances get other benefits. It was unimaginable for a Chinese person to understand this happening in a traditional capitalist country and was a big contrast to my prior understanding. In my school years, I was taught that capitalist countries exploit their workers in order to get maximum profit. At first, it was hard to understand how the government would so generously hand out so many benefits. By contrast, in socialist China, people do not get such generous state support (if there is any at all for rural residents) for housing, childcare and medical care.

My experience shows me that contemporary China is now a complex country rather than a simple socialist one. China is perhaps a more capitalist country than it was but with some hybrid socialist country characteristics, as described by Mann (2007). From different workplaces, I learned how British people treasure and fight for individual rights, as reflected in the number of industrial strikes and political campaigns which I witnessed over the years in the UK. Taking some recent events as examples, the British Airways industrial actions in 2010 forced the management to rethink its policy on cabin crew benefits, and the UK parliament had to review its members' expenses policy after a number of damaging news reports in 2009. From my observations, these were achieved mainly by respect for the law and legislation that protects individual rights. In China, there may be equivalent laws, but there appears to be lack of respect for them and their implementation. There are too many risks for individuals to campaign for their causes in China.

While studying in the UK, I realised that I have become more political and often unconsciously compare China with the outside world. The distance from my home country has actually brought me closer to it. I often think how China can become a more democratic and free society that respects and protects individual rights, while it develops its fast growing economy. I think about these issues not cynically but sincerely. It springs from my love for my birth place and my desire to make it a better place. Certainly, I am under no illusion that western capitalist political and economic systems are perfect examples for others to copy. No such illusion could survive after having witnessed the unpopular Iraq War as well as the recent collapse of financial markets, which many believed was caused by greedy capitalists – bankers in particular.

Becoming a research student

Immediately after completing my undergraduate degree, I was awarded a full scholarship to continue my studies at master's level. On completion of my master's degree in Computer Science, I was offered a job as IT Research and Support Specialist at the same university. I did not plan for further study at the time as I was thinking about my career. I had two choices – one was to go back to the IT industry and the other to work in the higher education sector, which I gradually found more attractive; I had already taught some undergraduate classes. In order to become an academic, it was essential to obtain a research degree and have a good research profile. After I determined to join the academic community, I gave some careful thought to a research proposal for a PhD degree.

The idea of conducting a research degree on Chinese undergraduate students' experiences in the UK came both from my personal interest in how I and other Chinese students were transformed by the experience, and from the importance of such research for UK higher education institutes. The doctoral research (Su, 2010) fulfils the requirements for a PhD degree of the University of Liverpool, while at the same time meeting the needs of the institution as a whole. It addresses one of the major priorities of the institution: the overriding need for the academic support of overseas students. The process of carrying out this research over a period of three years affected me both professionally and personally in a way which I did not foresee. Professionally, the process has changed my views on how to conduct social science research; personally, it made me realise how demanding a research degree could be for one's personal life. The birth of my daughter at the writing-up stage of my thesis certainly made the journey even more challenging and exciting.

I used to view research as based on hard data and the process of fact finding. However, because of the interdisciplinary nature of my doctoral study, it was designed to be empirically grounded, qualitative in methodological orientation, and socio-cultural in its conceptual framing. This was new to me as a researcher and it made me feel nervous since my previous postgraduate work had not entailed the kind of wide-ranging reading and theorising that is essential in social science research. I felt as though I had started a journey into an unfamiliar field. The first challenge was to construct a framework of analysis that (a) gathered what I saw to be the salient issues and questions, (b) guided and informed the analysis and (c) provided a tentative structure for the thesis as a whole.

When students of Chinese origin study as undergraduates in the UK, they encounter numerous unpredictabilities over and above the daunting unpredictabilities faced by indigenous students. Not only must they wrap their heads around their chosen discipline or field of study, but they must do this within an educational and cultural context which differs hugely from their own. They manage this transition in a second and in some cases a third language. Chinese students within the UK study in multiple, complicated, overlapping and sometimes contradictory contexts of learning. There was no ready-made framework which I could adopt for my chosen study. I had to construct that framework for myself – what the textbooks refer to as 'bricolage'.

I was fortunate to have an excellent research supervision team consisting of three professors in the field of higher education. They played a significant role in helping me with a number of challenging issues during the research. At the beginning of my doctoral study, I spent at least an hour each week in discussions with my principal PhD supervisor about how to develop a conceptual framework – or a kind of theoretical searchlight – to sustain and cast light on my study. I was also in regular email contact with the co-supervisors on specific aspects of my study. In the meetings with the principal supervisor, different theoretical perspectives were brought to bear on the research topic and gradually a set of research questions emerged. But we had to keep testing and re-testing these against the literature and our own understanding of the literature. This was a very challenging but exciting phase in the development of my enquiry.

The full account of constructing my conceptual framework is fully discussed in another book (Su *et al*, 2010). The process of the enquiry has made me realise that social science research is not linear, and it often starts with many uncertainties given the potential fuzziness of the study that is virtually limitless in its capacity for generating questions. As a new researcher, I have to learn to live with this. Another development was to realise the importance of reading – a wide-ranging survey of the relevant academic literatures. This is a demanding and difficult task but it is important for a researcher to understand how one's own field is related to other disciplines. For me, the scholarly interdisciplinary reading was the key for the construction of the framework of analysis for my research.

As a full-time PhD student working part-time and as a new parent, life during the three years of study was not easy. I managed to get a studentship from the university to cover the incredibly expensive tuition fees for overseas students (£10,000 per year). However, I still needed to work part-time to support my wife, myself and our daughter. Sometimes I worked twelve hours a day on my thesis and the job. I did not take any holidays and I always feel guilty at not having spent more time with my family. My wife's understanding and support made me work even harder in order to complete the study on time. As a result, I managed to complete the study six months early.

After many years' study in universities in both China and the UK, and achieving the highest possible academic qualification, I do not feel that I have learned everything in my chosen field of educational research. I am keen to continue my reading and thinking in the area of cross-cultural learning and the development of the learner within higher education settings, with particular reference to overseas students. Finding a job in the university sector as a lecturer was a dream for me, enabling me to pursue my career and academic interest.

Moving forward: my ongoing journey

After receiving my doctoral degree in 2010, I applied to a number of universities in the UK and received a job offer from Liverpool Hope University for a position as Post Doctoral Teaching Fellow in Education. It was a junior lecturer post with a focus on teaching undergraduate programmes and supervising some master dissertations in the area of education-related studies. As a new lecturer with English as my second language, teaching a cohort of 60 undergraduate students and supervising masters students was an enormous challenge for me. Changing my role from that of a research student to being a lecturer in a UK university was a difficult process, during which I learned some important lessons.

One lesson was how to communicate with students who are from a different culture, with a different educational background. It is crucial for me to be understood by students and make my message clear in the lecture. At the beginning, I was a bit worried that it might be a disadvantage for me to have English as my second language. As it turned out, language was not a big issue since I generally managed to speak slowly and clearly. My confidence in English has been gradually enhanced by presenting at conferences and delivering lectures to a large audience from time to time. Another lesson is how to utilise my international work and education experience for the benefit of students. Given my background of studying and working in two different countries, I am able to provide my students with different perspectives on many education issues in differing social-cultural contexts.

For me, teaching is both a challenging and an exciting profession. It is challenging because teaching is not only about practical skills but also a complex interaction between knowledge, theories, values and emotions demanding substantial engagement with learners; it is exciting because a lecturer can potentially have a positive influence on how students think and act in society. I have enjoyed teaching so far. Students' feedback has made me realise that I have had a very positive impact on their study and personal development.

Conclusion

Learning how to teach is still an ongoing journey – it is the learning of academic practice. My current dream is to learn how to make a difference in students' lives through teaching, and to make a contribution to the academic community and the wider public through research. I am delighted with what I have accomplished so far. I now hope to see the development of a more democratic China. Only when Chinese society becomes fairer and more equal, will more Chinese individuals like me make their dreams come true through their own efforts and intellectual development.

2

A Shanghainese solicitor in London: 'By endurance we conquer'

Jue Jun Lu

This chapter is organised around the places in which I have studied, worked and lived. The dates and times are not strictly sequential, so I can tell my tale with the benefit of hindsight, rather than following the straight arrow of time. This is not an autobiography. I attempt to cover only the most exciting, happy and miserable events of the seven years I have spent in the UK. I have never kept a diary and have therefore had to rely on my recollections in putting this memoir together. I have, however, endeavoured to check facts and verify details wherever possible.

As a girl, I had been dreaming of coming to the UK from the age of thirteen – the indefatigable British Royal Navy in the age of Nelson, dark Dickensian London full of gangs, villains, trials and tribulation, the marvellous strawberries and cream at Wimbledon – any one of these things was enough to lure me to the Empire on which the sun never set.

My education was always very important to my parents, particularly my father. During the Cultural Revolution he, a Shanghainese born and bred, was sent away to labour in rural Jiangxi Province for eleven years. His ordeal led him to believe that everything could disappear overnight, but if you still had your brains, education and drive, at least you could start over again! Given the world-class reputation of British education, coming to study in the UK was an obvious choice. But when to come over was hotly debated. Since at the time I already had a confirmed offer to study German at the Shanghai International Studies University (SISU)[1], my parents were adamant that I should wait until I finished university at home before venturing out to England. I was, however, too desperate to stay put. After over six months of persistent persuasion on my part, my parents gave in and I was allowed to turn down the offer from SISU and go to study in the UK after I finished school.

As regards what to study, my love for the English language rendered English literature a clear winner. Totally out of utilitarian motives, I decided also to study Spanish, delirious at the thought of being able to speak the second most widely spoken language in the world after Mandarin Chinese. In January 2003, I received an offer (somehow with no mention of a foundation course[2]) together with a scholarship of £1,000 a year from the University College Chester (as it then was) to read English and Spanish.

Finally, after nearly two years of arduous preparation, I landed on British soil on a clear September day almost seven years ago. I was eighteen then.

In Chester

Famous for its Rows and black-and-white architecture, Chester was one of the last towns to fall to the Normans in their conquest of England. The landmark city walls encircle the bounds of the medieval city and constitute the most complete city walls in Britain[3]. The College's campus is located just north of the city walls. It was here on the 32-acre campus that I started my learning journey.

The Heart of Darkness

The Heart of Darkness – first up on the reading list – was my first piece of homework. We were to read, analyse and appreciate Joseph Conrad's masterpiece in preparation for a 45-minute tutorial. Needless to say, the whole concept of 'tutorial' was alien to me: having just come through twelve years of schooling under the Chinese education system where taught classes were the primary, if not the only, means of teaching, I naturally thought the so-called 'tutorial' was simply the same wine in a different bottle.

Three days later, I was on my way to my first English tutorial. It was a beautiful autumn day. The morning sunlight shone gloriously on the city walls as if it wanted to illuminate their rich history. Passing briskly through various vantage points on the walls with striking views of the River Dee in the distance, I paused on the west side and could not take my eyes off the spectacular panoramas across to the Clwydian Hills of North Wales. Finally, coming off the wall on the northern side, I turned on to a narrow footpath through an avenue of gum trees and soon found myself outside a Victorian vicarage, which is the College's English Department.

Having settled down amongst a dozen young, eager faces, my thoughts finally focused on the tutorial itself. I thought about my preparation and felt an instant fit of nausea as I had no idea what Conrad's book was all about! Even though it was a short piece of merely 100-odd pages, it had been an impossible task. The mood was so dark, the prose so dense and the style so intense that however many times I read it through, I could not make the slightest sense of its basic plot, let alone its deeper meaning and literary value!

By this point, the tutorial had started and a blonde girl was speaking at an astounding speed about a certain part of the story; the next second an athletic-looking lad across the room butted in, then someone else spoke. Their voices whirled around in my head in a hopeless muddle. I stared at everyone's constantly moving lips, speechless. Over half an hour had passed before it suddenly occurred to me that I should also say something but I did not know what! Even if I had understood the book (which I had not), I concluded that with my command of English I was only going to make a complete fool of myself in front of the whole class. So I sat through the tutorial without uttering a word. Not daring to look the tutor in the eyes, I could nevertheless sense her scornful glances as I fled the room as soon as the tutorial was over.

Dragging my feet on the way back, I was boiling inside – I had always been the best throughout my primary and secondary schooling, but in that tutorial I knew, without a shadow of doubt, that I was bottom of the class. I felt my cheeks burning in the cold night air; I felt horribly ashamed.

17

Home, sweet home

During my time in Chester, I lived in a house in the centre of town, behind the elevated black-and-white Rows on Bridge Street and right by the famous Grosvenor Shopping Centre. The house accommodated the College's entire intake of international students, who were mostly Europeans on the Erasmus Programme. The house was an old three-storey brick building, bland and lacking in character. The inside was decorated in creamy white; it was austere and simple. There were seven bedrooms and two bathrooms on each floor along a narrow carpeted corridor, giving it a rather hotel-like feel. The shared kitchen was used as a common room.

In the house, Megan and Tania were my best friends. Megan was a tall, slim blonde girl with a wicked sense of humour and Tania was a typical Andalusian, open, fun and extremely friendly. In the morning, we would walk to College together, stopping at the cafe downstairs for coffee. In the evenings, Tania and Megan would always have a hearty meal ready to cheer me up after a long exhausting day at the College. In those very first days and weeks of my life in this country, their constant friendship filled me with the joy and warmth that was almost enough to fill the void in my heart left by the physical separation from my own family.

Being the only child in the family, I had been very close to and reliant upon my parents – having never been away from home for more than three days before coming to the UK, I had always been a tiny vulnerable chick under their wings. After the new sounds, sights and experiences had distracted me, the formalities of acquiring essentials kept me occupied for the first couple of weeks, and as life started to settle into a routine and the surroundings ceased to feel quite so exciting and exotic, the feeling of homesickness set in. Usually a sound sleeper, I started to go through times when I lay wide awake, longing desperately for the comforts of home. Not having a phone or laptop with me at the time, I had to resort to public computers in the College library to communicate with loved ones.

Dejected and weary from lack of sleep, I would nonetheless sit dutifully in the same spot in the library, logging on to my Hotmail account to check messages from home, which, owing to the College's uniform language input configuration, had to be written in Pinyin, the Romanised alphabetic form of Chinese. My brain instantly switched off at the sight of an incoming email from my parents, tears gushing down uncontrollably. Unable to cope with my overwhelming sadness and misery, I would often sit sobbing quietly for hours, totally oblivious to the students and staff walking past me. Sailing away from England on his first Antarctic expedition, Sir Ernest Shackleton, the well known Edwardian explorer, put very aptly this overpowering sense of homesickness during long separation in a poem to his wife,

> My hand in writing falters
> My eyes grow dim with tears
> For long long days are before us
> To be filled with hopes and fears... [4]

Realising it was already dark, I would get up to go home, back to my tiny room in the Bridge Street house. Longing for the other home thousands of miles away, I heard someone sing,

> Home, sweet home.
> To thee I'll return
> Home, home, sweet, sweet home
> There's no place like home, oh, there's no place like home!

Estudié Español

The College's Spanish degree programme had two entry cohorts; I was allocated to the one which required no prior knowledge of the language. All the teaching was delivered by means of small class tutorials – fifteen students sitting around an oak horseshoe table leaving the tutor and a whiteboard in the middle. Away from the table, twenty-odd computer work stations were lined up against the walls, the majority still having the same exercise open on the screen, indicating that the students had just finished their Spanish listening practice. In the far left corner of the room stood two wooden bookshelves stuffed with books, dictionaries, CDs and other resources. The tutor, Mark, a lanky man in his early thirties, was explaining the regular verb conjugations in the Spanish past tense. Mark, who had spent ten years in Spain first as an exchange student and then as a teaching assistant at a college in Valencia, had undoubtedly picked up the Southern Spanish warmth and openness-he was an incredibly nice person and an excellent tutor.

Compared to learning English, Spanish was a far greater challenge, not least because I was 18 instead of 11 when I started. Not only was Spanish grammar much more complex (with its two-gender noun system, regular and irregular verb conjugations and the noun and pronominal declension), pronouncing the Spanish R proved to be totally impossible. On top of all these obstacles, all my Spanish lessons were taught in English, which (for the first three months at least) effectively meant that I could either put on a brave face and keep nodding my head or press my head as low against my chest as possible, praying that Mark would not pick on me.

Even though I was right out of my comfort zone, I loved every minute of my Spanish classes! Whilst others may find the whole process of learning a foreign language unbearably tedious, I was greatly interested and loved nothing more than gradually getting to grips with the puzzling grammar rules and exploring and grasping the often subtle semantic differences between words.

Often I wondered how I could have enjoyed my Spanish classes so much and yet been so indifferent to the English modules. I had no answer until I went to my last English poetry class in which we studied one of Shakespeare's sonnets –

> Thine eyes I love, and they, as pitying me,
> Knowing thy heart torments me with disdain,
> Have put on black and loving mourners be,
> Looking with pretty ruth upon my pain.
> And truly not the morning sun of heaven
> Better becomes the grey cheeks of the east,
> Nor that full star that ushers in the even
> Doth half that glory to the sober west,
> As those two mourning eyes become thy face:
> O, let it then as well beseem thy heart
> To mourn for me, since mourning doth thee grace,
> And suit thy pity like in every part.
> Then will I swear beauty herself is black
> And all they foul that thy complexion lack[5]

I was completely stunned by the poem. Apparently, the speaker loves his lady's eyes even as they look at him 'with disdain'; sunrise and sunset do not beautify the land so well as her 'two mourning eyes' glorify her face. The sun that is 'usher[ing] in' evening is a 'full star,' but it offers less than 'half the glory' that the lady's eyes give to her face. In the couplet, the speaker decides to accept the situation and even support the woman for her beauty. Unfortunately, the idea that beauty is a beauty eludes this speaker and he continues to look past the pain she causes him as long as he can enjoy her beauty[6].

I sat alone in silence for a long time after the tutorial, hopelessly confused. I could not see why my brain just would not conjure up the slightest clue about 'the full star that ushers in the even' or 'the morning sun of heaven'. For the previous two months, I had been struggling to figure out why I was unable to observe the most obvious sentiments in the plainest and crudest ways of expression and this was just another prime example of my failings. In a split second, it dawned on me that perhaps I just did not have the disposition of mind and imagination to appreciate the beauty and subtlety of literature, as Phillip Carey[7] lacked the artistic talent to be anything more than a mediocre painter. By this point, I had come to accept my own limitations and was neither upset nor ashamed about my unsatisfactory performance in the English modules. I was not sorry either to have spent a year studying literature only to find out that it was not for me – I had learned enough about myself in the process to justify the time spent and expenses incurred – but I was not going to go on with something at which I knew I was no good. I decided to give up English Literature immediately and go down another route – law – which I had thought worth attempting from the start but failed to take up for fear of appearing conventional. I had an inkling that my scientific and almost meticulous brain would be well suited to that discipline, which is known to place considerable emphasis on logic, precision and thoroughness.

With first class grades from Chester, I expected to receive an offer from Liverpool Law School and I did.

Liverpool years

During my three years in Liverpool, one of the most memorable scenes will always be that June night in 2005 when, after winning the European Champions League title, the Liverpool footballers toured the city centre in a double-decker bus among a sea of Reds fans. Liverpool was buzzing; hundreds of thousands of fans filled the streets to applaud their heroes' performance in Istanbul – it was a truly sensational night!

A law degree

I first harboured an ambition for law after seeing Tom Cruise's *A Few Good Men*. I finally got into law school some six years later, by which point it had become a fixed dream of mine to become a lawyer.

In the UK, lawyers are divided into solicitors and barristers who perform different tasks in what is called a split profession[8]. An academic qualification in law is not a licence to practise as a lawyer; aspiring solicitors must also undertake the applicable vocational training course[9] and complete a training contract[10] before they can be admitted as fully qualified solicitors, and would-be barristers need to undertake their relevant vocational training (which is the Bar Vocational Course) before they are called to the Bar (meaning in effect that the professional qualification to practise as a barrister is granted) and complete a pupilage[11] to establish themselves in the profession.

Being Chinese, I knew from the outset that it would be a fight whichever route I chose to go down – I would not only have to overcome stringent immigration controls (as a result of which many law firms and barristers' chambers simply do not consider applications from non-European nationals[12]) but also beat off fierce competition from tens of thousands of fellow students from top universities (including Oxbridge graduates[13]). The odds were stacked overwhelmingly against me and I knew I had to aim high.

I had always known that law was a difficult subject but it was not until my first couple of weeks on the course were over that I realised just how tough it was. While I remain sceptical whether the scare tactics that the then LLB programme leader, Ms Norris, deployed throughout my first ever law lecture were conducive to learning, I very quickly realised that they were not completely devoid of truth – the law degree is, relatively and absolutely speaking, hard, requiring both raw knowledge and high-level analytical skills. Not only would one have to wade through large amounts of statutes and case law to ascertain the correct legal position, one must also fit the law to the factual scenarios at hand. Coming from an education background that strives always for the right answer, I was totally amazed to find that there is simply no such thing as a 'right' answer in law – as a lawyer, you are meant to make the argument as it suits your case – the fine line that divides success from failure hinges largely, if not entirely, on how convincingly the former is constructed on the basis of the latter.

But before I arrived at these observations, I was dazed by the material (and its sheer volume) with which I had to grapple. After wandering around the university bookshop, I bought fourteen textbooks for the first semester and found that more than ten of them had spines three inches thick. Sitting down to read for my first tutorial, I was hit by 121 new words on the first page of my Public Law textbook! Turning to the first case referenced on the reading list, I was disheartened to see that the judgment was crammed with Latin, of which I knew not a word. Undeterred by all these seemingly insurmountable obstacles, I totally immersed myself in what was before me. With my still passionate love for linguistics, I was eager to learn the highly technical legal vocabulary and explore the various specialised ways in which colloquial terms are used in legal settings.

Although plodding through page after page of dry legal texts was mind-numbingly boring, I persevered. Gradually, I found myself spending more and more time with the books themselves rather than with the dictionary and the originally incomprehensible judgments and statutes somehow grew clear. I knew I was making progress and was elated at each perceptible improvement. At the end of my first year, the criminal law examination took the form of a 3000-word essay on the meaning and judicial interpretation of 'recklessness' and I managed to get one of the highest marks awarded across the law school. This was the first time I truly believed that despite all the apparent adversities I could still triumph over the other 265 students in my year and be one of the Law School's very best – what a thought that was!

The course became much more challenging in the second year: not only were the likes of Equity and Trust Law much harder than any of the first year subjects, the workload had become incredibly heavy. Tired of making burgers and selling football shirts and trainers, I had, by the end of my first year, found myself a job at the Liverpool Royal Hospital working as a medical records clerk. Having to work every day between

5 and 8 in the evening, I was struggling to stick to the Law School's whopping 60-hour recommended weekly study time. Knowing that I could no longer afford to linger nonchalantly over my studies, I determinedly went about training myself to work more efficiently and purposefully in the precious time I had. I set myself a target reading time and made a conscious effort to stay focused, however dry and tedious the work before me was. Whether this self-training was successful I do not know; suffice to say that I managed everything, just about.

The weeks ahead of my third year finals were, without a shadow of doubt, the hardest and most trying time of my life. Although I had had a solid second year in terms of academic results, I would nevertheless need an impeccable third year record to secure that all-important degree classification. Rushing manically between my studies and the hospital job, various voluntary positions and law school commitments, I was unable to start revision properly until normal teaching had ceased, which meant that I had less than three weeks to ready myself for five challenging law exams.

Knowing full well that I had a headlong race against time, I was ruthlessly strict with myself – my day would start punctually at 7.30 and finish at 1.30 the following morning; I gauged exactly how much time was needed for meals, washing and sleeping and devoted the remainder of my waking hours to revision. Sustained by excessive caffeine, I sat rigidly at my desk for almost twenty hours every day, slogging through a staggering amount of paper and trying with all my might to memorise the two thousand odd cases that were required for each exam. The going got tougher and tougher as the days passed and after my third exam I felt physically and mentally exhausted. Repeating to myself the family motto of Sir Ernest Shackleton: 'By endurance we conquer', I urged myself to go on. It subsequently transpired that I was one of only six out of 265 students awarded a first class law degree that year.

On a sunny day, a month after the exams had finished, I attended my graduation ceremony with my parents and was finally in possession of the piece of paper for which I had worked so hard for the previous three years. My brain was very confused – I was relieved, proud and deeply satisfied. But most overwhelming of all the feelings in my heart was 'a perfect contentment that comes of work accomplished'.[14]

International student of the year

Somehow, I always had the feeling that the areas around Liverpool were relatively less affluent than the rest of the UK and this feeling could not have been more emphatically conformed by the days and months I spent volunteering at the local Citizens Advice Bureau (CAB).

The CAB was situated on the first floor of a shabby grey building in Liverpool city centre. Going through the front door, immediately facing me was a tiny desk on which stood two or three double-tier trays stuffed with papers and leaflets, where the receptionist would sit. In front of this was a square meeting area with plastic chairs lined up against two walls and a narrow corridor on the left hand side along which were half a dozen drab meeting rooms.

CAB staff and volunteers all worked in an open plan office area separated from the crowd of advice-seekers by a keypad door. Still a full-time law student, I squeezed one day a week out of my university schedules to volunteer as a legal advisor at the CAB. Not only were the matters I dealt with at the CAB wide-ranging, but the people I helped came from all walks of life. Most of the time, I had welfare enquiries where less well-off members of the public came for help to enable them to go or stay on the dole. Every now and then I had clients with debt problems. Often I was shocked at the extent to which some had got themselves into the red and yet deeply saddened by the circumstances in which they had tried but failed to shake off the shackles they had put on themselves.

Once I received an elderly lady, Anne, from a rather run-down area just outside Liverpool. She must have been in her eighties, speaking with a trembling voice and looking rather fragile. Her only son had emigrated to the United States and she was living on her own. After nearly an hour spent going through the receipts, documents and letters that Anne had rummaged for in the three Tesco bags she brought with her, I got a vague idea of the case – Anne had purchased an electric heater the previous winter worth £65. Although she had been paying back small sums over the past year (which amounted to well over £200 in total), penalty charges and interest over the unpaid debt had been accruing continually and had reached £556. Having ignored numerous letters and warnings, she now had bailiffs banging on her door every couple of days threatening to force their way in and seize her furniture.

I was shaken and stirred by her story – I was angry that a helpless elderly person like Anne could be put through such hardship and my heart ached to think that she had had to leave her house before 6 o'clock that morning to avoid being caught by the ambushing bailiffs. I sprang into action immediately; phone calls and letters ensued. After two weeks of arduous effort, I managed to get the credit company to write off the remainder of the sum owed and cancel their collection instructions to the bailiffs. All in all, it was a happy ending. Another week later, Anne came in to the CAB again. Still weak and slow in her movement, she had a glow of radiance in her cheeks. She had baked some of my favourite blueberry muffins to thank me. I was more than surprised; I was stunned and speechless. I was overjoyed. But stronger and more over-whelming than joy was a distinct sense of fulfilment – the satisfaction I felt at the thought that I had changed someone else's life for the better was beyond description. It was one of the proudest moments of my life.

Liverpool University, like many others up and down the country, had a Widening Participation (WP) programme, funded by the Labour govern-ment, to attempt to increase participation in Higher Education, parti-cularly by students from so-called 'non-traditional' backgrounds (for example, students from lower income families, disabled students, stu-dents from ethnic minority groups and mature students). From the second year onwards, I became involved in a number of WP initiatives. During term-time, we organised Open Days to show pupils from local state schools around the university campus, arranged for them to meet students with similar upbringing and generally tried to instil in their young hearts and minds some goals and aspirations. We also ran out-reach projects whereby some university students were sent to local schools to engage with the pupils there and raise the profile of Higher Education.

While all of these projects had been fun and interesting, my favourite was definitely the Aimhigher Summer School Programme, which was designed to give young people a taste of university life and help them decide whether to apply for Higher Education and, if so, what to study. Typically, over two weeks in the summer, young people, accommodated in Liverpool University's Dale Hall, would explore a range of academic subjects through group work and lectures and learn about financing further study and career opportunities for graduates. During those bright summer days, I learned from those teenagers much more than the convoluted rules of cricket (which I still do not fully understand). Their lives, experiences and backgrounds provided a wider perspective on the social components of British society, which was perhaps my first step towards truly assimilating into the country in which I had lived for almost two years.

In early 2005, my finances were in dire straits. Having infuriated my father the summer before with my 'flippant whim'[15] to give up English Literature and study law, I had not received a penny from him since the start of that academic year. Although the modest income from the hospital job was enough to cover my living expenses, I was short of funds for the next instalment of my tuition fees which would become due in April. By a happy coincidence, on one of the Law School's notice boards I stumbled across an advert for the British Council's Shine International Student of the Year Award competition. It was open to international students across the country and the winner (usually out of thousands of applicants) received a prize of £1000. I entered the competition with a short essay on my life and experiences since coming to the UK. A letter arrived three weeks later and took me by complete surprise. It said that I had been selected out of 2,354 entrants as a finalist for the Shine Award and that I was invited to a final round of interviews in London, following which an award ceremony would be held.

I cannot recall exactly how I got through the interviews, presentation and filming; all I remember is that I had been sitting at the fabulous award ceremony hosted by Channel 4's Krishnan Guru-Murthy for what seemed a lifetime. Suddenly my name was called out and instantaneously the sun broke through – it was as if all the gloom, depression and anxiety had been lifted off my shoulders and life was bright, beautiful and hopeful again. In remembrance of that magical moment, I keep a photo of me holding the shiny trophy, beaming at the side of the former Labour leader, Neil Kinnock.

Predictably, my father and I were reconciled soon after I returned to Liverpool – he decided that I was old enough to take care of my own business and that it was high time that he let go of the tight control over my life to which he had always felt entitled. Finally and for the first time in my life, I felt that I was my own master and that the life ahead of me was truly bright, beautiful and hopeful!

City lawyer

Having finished the vocational course at BPP Law School, I went travelling around South America and the Antarctic for five months. It was not until January 2009 that I finally started my training contract at a City law firm. Although the world was in the middle of a recession and business was slow, I found the transition from law student to trainee solicitor abrupt and breath-taking. Unlike academics – most of whom love to sit on the fence – lawyers in practice are often in the habit of adopting a direct and no-nonsense approach to legal advice. I was therefore no longer tested on the academic merit in my legal analysis or how well both sides of the argument were balanced; instead, what mattered was how the products and services I provided helped to solve the client's problem, both legally and commercially.

In addition to the difference in thinking and attitude, the hours which the job of a City lawyer entails caught me off guard. It was far from un-common that I found myself still slaving away in the office well after the day was technically over and, with the advent of the Blackberry, there was little guarantee of a work-free weekend either. Thankfully, I some-how fairly quickly got used to the fast-paced, work-oriented life as a City lawyer.

Now nearing the end of my training contract, I am a timid lawyer no longer; I am on my way to becoming a capable, fluent legal practitioner. Unsure of what the future holds, I must nevertheless stride on, brave and confident.

Epilogue

Now, I have almost told all there is to tell about my life and experiences in the UK to date. Looking ahead, I see myself, with loved ones at my side, following the long road of life. As I travel on, I am sure to encounter new events and meet new people. But whichever turn I take along the way, I know the learning journey will continue for as long as I live.

Such is my journey; such is life.

Notes

1 A brief introduction to the Shanghai International Studies University is available at http://language.shisu.edu.cn/English/about_shisu.html

2 This is a one-year university preparation course which overseas students are usually required to complete before they are offered a degree course. The course is a bridge between overseas students' current qualifications and UK University undergraduate entry requirements.

3 A brief introduction to Chester can be found at http://www.chester360.co.uk/chester-the-walled-city.htm

4 Ernest Shackleton, an Anglo-Irish man, was an Edwardian explorer whom I idolised to the point of worship. This quotation is from E. H. Shackleton, letter to Emily Shackleton, 6 November 1907; R. Huntford, *Shackleton,* Abacus, 1996, p191

5 William Shakespeare, Sonnet 132 CXXXII

6 More analysis of this sonnet can be found at http://british-poetry.suite101.com/article.cfm/shakespeare_sonnet_132

7 Phillip Carey is the main character in *Of Human Bondage* by William Somerset Maugham. I happened to be reading the novel at the time and found Phillip's revelations regarding his artistic gift (or rather the lack of it) and his self-exploration leading up to his decision to give up studying art most instructive.

8 Solicitors' work covers a broad range, including advising commercial and private clients on business matters and property and undertaking litigation, whereas most barristers' work is confined to litigation and they make their living primarily through advocacy. For more information on the differences between these two branches see http://business.timesonline.co.uk/tol/business/law/article1061175.ece

9 Having obtained a law degree or its equivalent, which may be achieved through a combination of a non-law degree and a Graduate Diploma in Law (which is a postgraduate law course allowing non-law graduates to convert to law after university), would-be solicitors need to complete a one-year vocational course, known as the Legal Practice Course, whereas the barrister's course, also lasting for one academic year, is called the Bar Vocational Course.

10 The training contract is the final stage on the path to qualifying as a solicitor in the UK. It is a two-year apprenticeship undertaken at a law firm, at the end of which the trainee solicitor in question can apply to the Law Society to be admitted as a qualified solicitor.

11 A pupilage is the last stage of training to be a barrister in England and Wales. It is similar to an apprenticeship where the pupil shadows an experienced barrister to gain hands-on experience and usually lasts one year.

12 However, law firms which flatly refuse to consider training contract applications from students who would require a work permit have been forced to reconsider their policies, after the Employment Appeals Tribunal upheld a finding of indirect race discrimination on the grounds of nationality in *Osborne Clarke v. Purohit* in February 2009.

13 Recent Legal Week research found that Oxbridge graduates made up 38% of trainee solicitors at the Magic Circle firms (which is an informal term used to describe collectively or any one of the five leading London-based law firms, namely Clifford

Chance, Allen + Overy, Slaughter and May, Freshfields Bruckhaus Deringer and Link-laters) over the last two years. More details can be found at http://www.legalweek.com/legal-week/blog-post/1598461/oxbridgers-city-unbridgeable-divide

14 Hunsford, R (1996) *Shackleton*, p593

15 Even to this day, my stubborn father will still refer to my decision to switch to law as a flippant whim, although he now admits that my 'whim' has, by some lucky chance, paid off!

3

A Chinese academic in a Welsh
university: luck, reality, dream

Anwei Feng

This chapter focuses on my personal experience of the transformation of my world views in the academy – the higher education institutions – I have worked in. Before I came to the UK in
1989, I had been greatly affected by all the major political events in
China, from the Great Leap Forward movement in the late 1950s, the
Cultural Revolution, and Deng Xiaoping's initial return to power in the
early 1970s, to the active implementation of his 'reform and open-door'
policies in the post-Mao era. Most effects were disheartening, but some
were positive. Since the end of the Cultural Revolution, through studying, working and living in different tertiary institutions in China, the UK
and other countries, I have sensed some fundamental changes in my
perspectives in viewing the world and thus my aims or goals in life,
teaching and research.

I begin with my earliest childhood memories. As a boy, growing up in a
socio-economically deprived family, I experienced much hardship and
received poor education. The reality was harsh. Against all the odds, I
was lucky enough to enter a university. There follows a detailed account
of the life dreams I chased, first in China and then in the UK, from a
dream to shed a scandalous identity historically created, to the ambition to obtain a PhD that took me a decade to realise by living and
working in four different countries and regions, to more dreams that
have made me what I am today. Some of the stories of my life are

explicable in psychological and socio-economic terms but, being a generally motivated academic living in the rapidly-changing world in the last half-century, my other stories have to be understood with more than straightforward logic.

Hunan Nga Zi (Hunan kid)

Because of a widespread famine caused primarily by the Great Leap Forward movement[1], I moved at the age of 5 with my parents from a small village in Hunan Province to Wuhan, the capital city of Hubei. Living in a rather poor neighbourhood where there were quite a number of Hunan migrant families like ours, I got to know some children of these families and was able to speak the Hunan dialect for quite some time. Needless to say, I was sometimes bullied by the local street kids there. In a fight with a local boy of similar age, in which I got the upper hand, the boy ran away shouting *'Hunan Nga Zi, Bie Nga Zi ...'* (Hunan kid, son of a ...) in Hunan dialect with a Wuhan accent. Instead of feeling happy with the win, I burst into tears. Boys use bad language in these situations, of course. What hurt me most was not the language but the skilful way he employed it to infuriate me. *Bie Nga Zi* was not a swearword used in that Wuhan street, but a common curse used by us Hunan children to insult each other when we were angry. Knowing my identity and knowing the Hunan curse, the boy mocked my low-status Hunan migrant identity as well. Within six months or so after that incident, I managed to speak perfect Wuhanese, the local dialect, by completely eradicating my Hunan accent. I was pleased to note that the boys in the neighbourhood would then use the local foul language in our fights.

This is by no means an unusual story. Many migrant or immigrant children in the world may well have had similar experiences. What makes this story special to me is the fact that from an early age I became keenly aware of one's linguistic identity in relation to self-esteem and developed a deep interest in languages/dialects and language learning to negotiate my place in society. This episode has remained in my memory so vividly that I feel justified in claiming that it has had a huge influence on some life choices I have made and research interests I have developed in my teaching career.

Two surprises – pure luck?

As a migrant family, my parents had to work very hard to make ends meet. Having lived in the city of Wuhan for some time, my father found a job in a chemical factory in the suburbs and moved the whole family there. My mother had to do some part-time jobs in the factory to help feed a family of four children and our old grandfather. Living conditions were harsh and many people in the neighbourhood were like us with only one earner in the house, and were thus socially and economically deprived. There was a school affiliated to the factory. It was a small converted building which had formerly been used as workers' dormitories, so the classrooms were very small with limited facilities. Most teachers were simply selected from the factory staff as having received relatively more education than ordinary workers. Despite the school's poor resources, the teachers and school leaders kept reminding us that life was much better than it had been before the 'liberation' in 1949 when the People's Republic of China was founded. Therefore, we should treasure the happy life and study hard.

My elder brother did study very hard. With surprisingly good exam results in that harsh environment, he managed to move to a reputable secondary school in the city when he finished primary school in the factory. He became a role model for me and for all the other kids in the school. I often dreamed of following in his footsteps to attend a proper secondary school in the city after primary school. However, I had no chance to do this as the Great Cultural Revolution broke out in 1966 before I finished primary school.

Having spent the first three years – mostly at home with limited schooling in the initial period of the Cultural Revolution, I had to prepare myself at the age of 15 to go to a village in the countryside to receive re-education from the peasants, that is, to answer the call of the then paramount leader, Mao Zedong. To our great surprise, however, some traditional academically-oriented secondary schools resumed recruiting students in 1969 after the worst riots in the first three years of the Revolution. I was chosen by the school leaders to continue my senior secondary education in one of the best schools in Wuhan, thanks mainly to my poor worker's family background (the so-called proletarian class during the Mao era) and perhaps to my modest personality as well. I could see that this was a huge relief for my parents as my elder brother, who had been so outstanding academically, had already been sent to the country and was having a very hard time in a village in the remote, mountainous part of the province. I was used to seeing my mother's tears whenever she had to bid farewell to my brother, but now at least some smiles came back to her with me around at weekends. She often said that I would be the most cultured person in the family.

After two years in senior secondary school, something even more astonishing happened to me. I was selected by the leaders of my secondary school to enter quite a well-known university to study foreign languages. The selection criteria might have been similar to those used two years earlier, but the process was in no way transparent. While we were overjoyed, my family simply could not believe this because no one in the family had the political power or social connections to make this happen. It is widely known that social connections and/or power have always been two major forms of social capital to make things work in China. My being chosen to enter a university in the early 1970s was seen as a myth or a miracle by many including ourselves; the simple fact was that most of my classmates were from socio-politically privileged backgrounds.

Based on my own reflections and the literature on that particular period, my own conclusion is that some people with power, such as the leaders of my school and the university that recruited me, were still idealistic because of political indoctrination with Mao's socialist ideals during the Cultural Revolution. Some of them were still taking equity and social representation into account when it came to decision-making for life opportunities. This was subtly shown by the fact that, before the selection, a leader from my secondary school and a Party secretary from the university that recruited me had visited my family in that suburban chemical factory. The sympathetic looks on their faces and the kind voice used to talk to my parents are still vivid in my memory.

A professional career

Unlike the then predominant 'worker-peasant-soldier' students[2] in the university, we, the foreign language majors, found ourselves a minority group because we were learning foreign languages which had been strongly attacked as they were associated with imperialism and bour-geois ideology. In addition, unlike them, we had not worked in factories, or on farms, or joined the army. However, later on, we got to know that, in some other important universities in the country, there were many foreign language majors like us. The recruitment of the relatively large number of foreign language majors was usually seen as a precursor of Deng Xiaoping's initial return to political power. As a reformer, he saw the need to maintain and raise the level of foreign language education and prepared us as future foreign language educators for facilitating his 'open-door' strategy, once he came to in power. Nonetheless, as univer-sity students at that time, we were naturally seen by the 'worker-peasant-soldier' students and society in general as rare species that did not belong there.

Despite the situation and poor foreign language resources[3] and despite being late starters in foreign language learning, we all treasured univer-sity life and quickly acquired the two foreign languages – Japanese and English – which we were taught. My progress was rapid due to my parti-cular interest in languages, strong motivation in language learning, and above all my foreign language learner identity that I felt very proud of. I still remember proudly practising speaking English or Japanese in public places, such as on a bus or in a canteen. After graduation, in the post-Mao era, like most of my classmates, I stayed on in that university as an English instructor.

Because of the severe shortage of English teaching personnel, we played a major role in offering English language courses at various levels in the initial 'open-door' era. We all seemed to shine in teaching for the simple reason that we had better English pronunciation than many of our senior colleagues, most of whom had been Russian teachers by training before the Cultural Revolution and had to trans-form themselves into English teachers through short training courses after the Revolution. As young, properly trained English teachers, we were popular as we were able to teach language courses, including spoken English, to all levels of learners, whether they were under-graduate or postgraduate students, or staff members who wished to learn English. Most of our senior colleagues could only cope with basic-level undergraduate classes using the traditional grammar-translation approach and many of them were not able to teach oral English. I remember regularly receiving awards for 'outstanding' performance in teaching and being promoted from teaching assistant to lecturer after a few years of teaching. Life looked good for the *Hunan Nga Zi*.

The twist – the reality leading to a dream

The easy life in the early 1980s didn't last long. The country began to open its doors wider and wider to the outside world as the decade progressed, and more and more students and staff members I had taught or trained were going abroad for further studies or as visiting scholars. For a poor country that had been closed to the outside world for so long, that was a dream which everybody was chasing. The socio-economic prestige and academic respect enjoyed by the returnees with a western degree or western academic experience became more and more evident. 'Outstanding' as I was, I never seemed to stand a chance. It soon became clear that society broadly categorised us as the products of the Cultural Revolution, the same as the 'worker-peasant-soldier' students, who were of lower quality than those educated in the post-Mao era. I saw the perceived advantages gradually slip away as society changed. To have a future, the best way was to to go abroad to study, to work, or even just to visit. The rapidly changing society seemed to value all things foreign and look up to people who were 'gold plated' (*dujing*) with foreign experience.

During the 1980s, it was almost impossible for Chinese lecturers to study abroad at their own expense as the salary for a lecturer was the equivalent of about US$10 per month (RMB97 per month in my case, as I clearly remember). The prospects of getting a scholarship for a language teaching degree from a western higher education institution were almost zero. During that time, opportunities to go abroad usually depended on official agreements reached at the state or institutional level and the people who went abroad were mostly co-sponsored by foreign institutions and the education authorities at various levels in China. Therefore, chances to go abroad were rare and were keenly competed for by all capable academic and administrative staff in education or research institutions during the two decades of the Deng Xiaoping era. These opportunities were usually taken directly by deans, department heads or others in similar positions, and then by those who were in favour with the people in power and in the right positions. It was said that there was a secret ranking of 'well-behaved' people kept by the leaders in each department for these precious opportunities.

In a gigantic foreign languages department of more than 100 teachers who all wished to be sent abroad, my dream remained a dream for a long time. I was neither a person in power nor did I have useful social connections at home or in the wider world. Power and social connections, unfortunately, appeared to have become the pillars of society and surprises like the ones I had experienced before would never happen again.

Grasping a rare chance

An opportunity finally came when the department I was in unexpectedly held an open competition by examination for two staff to go abroad. This decision was made not because the leaders suddenly became more open-minded and wanted the system to be fairer and more transparent, but because the sponsoring party – the British Council – required that the candidates pass the IELTS scores before doing an MA programme in Britain. I guess not many on their secret list could possibly do well enough to satisfy the British Council's requirement, so clearly a wise option would be to hold an open competition in order to choose the candidates who were likely to pass the then relatively new IELTS examination, which was said to be more difficult than the popular TOEFL[4].

This opportunity was given to all the English teachers in the department, including a few who had already left the department to do their MA degrees at other universities, because they were still on the payroll. The test was to be held soon after the department announced its decision. I felt strongly that this might be a chance that would never repeat itself. The initial selection test to be taken in the department was the key, as all those who perceived themselves as competent would be there to try their luck. Quite a number of bright young teachers in the department were clearly in a more advantageous position than me either in terms of age or with regard to length of training. So my preparation had to be thorough and strategic. Against all the odds, I stood out in the test among quite a sizeable group of contenders. In the subsequent formal IELTS examination held in Beijing, my scores both in overall competence and in the individual elements were satisfactory and my dream of going abroad to do a degree finally came true.

The primary goal

Like numerous other Chinese scholars and students in the 1980s, I cheerfully left my parents and my own family behind in October 1989, right after the events in Tiananmen Square (and of course I underwent quite a long period of political studies in Beijing before departure). Separation from my family was accepted willingly by everyone like me as a necessary sacrifice, as going abroad was believed to lead to a better life. On the plane to London, I recall that there were a large number of individuals like me and most, if not all, felt very fortunate to be able to get out of the country and were excited to be pursuing their dreams abroad. Many of today's Chinese students may find that very difficult to understand or even believe.

The purpose of my study abroad was crystal clear, to get rid of a historically created 'scandalous' identity by earning a respected degree. By doing a degree in which all modules were taught by native speakers of English, it was assumed that near-perfect competence in the English language would be acquired automatically. The combination of a proper degree and near-native speaker competence would ensure social prestige and respect in a Chinese higher education institution.

The course I took was entitled MA in Applied and Descriptive Linguistics, offered by Essex University, near Colchester. As the Language and Linguistics Department was one of the best in the UK, we were taught by a high quality team of linguists, some of whom were world famous, such as theoretical linguists, Andrew Radford and Vivian Cook, and sociolinguist/dialectologist, Peter Trudgil. They were indeed all well-respected scholars and inspired me to work exceptionally hard for every module I took in the one-year study. During the course, I developed a deep interest in sociolinguistics, the relationship between language and society, and did my dissertation under the supervision of Peter Trudgil.

Using psychological terms, I developed both intrinsic motivation, a deep interest in the language and in language study in general, and extrinsic motivation, the explicit goal for gaining a 'real degree' in order to win myself good 'face'[5] and an easy life. My MA course turned out to be more than successful. In a group of a dozen or so students, some of whom were English native speakers, I was one of the two who finished the MA course with distinction. This was not something that might cause a stir among my friends in the UK, but it surprised many people in my home university in Wuhan, China. I was naturally very proud of myself and was eager to return to the university to show off my MA with distinction certificate; I was looking forward to a return to an easy life on that campus.

A higher reverie

In the early 1990s, everything in China seemed to start changing even more rapidly, including people's way of thinking. 'Why do you wish to go back since you have done so well in Essex? There are so many wanting to get out', said a colleague-cum-friend in China. 'You should try to get a PhD there before thinking about coming back. In the not-too-distant future, MA degree holders will be everywhere', he continued. Indeed, with the general hunger for university degrees in China and the social prestige and power that go with them, a British PhD degree is something worthwhile. The tendency – viewed by many as corrupt – of some Chinese universities to award higher degrees for financial gain or on the basis of social connections made western degrees even more prestigious. Since I showed some academic potential as a researcher or scholar, why should I not stay on and do a PhD in a British university?

I researched my new plan. While my MA was done in a fairly straight-forward fashion as I was sponsored by a British Council studentship, doing a PhD looked virtually impossible because of the lack of financial resources. Full scholarships were rare in my specialised area. The only financial support I could apply for was the Overseas Research Student-ship (ORS), which would cover the difference in tuition fees between British and overseas students. I tried and succeeded, but eventually gave up because I still had to find the rest of the money to pay for fees and my living expenses. Through working part time in a Burger King restaurant, I learned how difficult it could be to make ends meet. However, I did not give up the dream. It was for this new dream that I started a long journey, one that would thoroughly transform my life and world views, and the lives of my whole family.

A 'sojourner' with a hidden task

In describing this part of my journey, I wish to use the term 'sojourner', because by and large it reflects my work and life in three different cultural settings after my MA study in the UK. This term usually refers to a person who spends a substantial period of time in a foreign country with the intention of returning at some point to his home culture (Furnham, 1988). The sojourner always has a specific task in mind and tends to interact with the locals to the extent that this helps to get the job done (Siu, 1952). By this definition I was a sojourner during those years, even though, in retrospect, my intention to stay only temporarily changed gradually as my interactions with the host culture deepened with the passing of time.

A clear priority was to obtain the necessary funding for my PhD study. As scholarships were hard to come by, I turned to the job market. I was an English language teacher by profession, but it was difficult to get such a job in the UK. One day, when I was reading a newspaper, I noticed an advertisement for English language teachers to teach in a national university in a country in the Middle East. The job looked very much like the one I had been doing in China with a decent salary, other benefits and a flexible, one year renewable contract. I applied and got the job. Determined as I was, I accepted the job and ended up in Qatar. This became the formal starting point for me as a sojourner in search of an answer to a dilemma.

My wife and daughter soon joined me in Qatar and we started a new life in a country that differed hugely from China in language, culture and life style. We were provided with a spacious apartment by the university, with almost no bills to pay except for international phone calls. We soon made friends with some expatriate colleagues working in the same university and the small Chinese community including the Chinese Embassy staff. Life was relatively easy and after one year the contract was renewed without a hitch. However, as a sojourner, I did not forget my mission and kept an eye on opportunities. At a seminar held in the department, I got to know Mike Byram from Durham University in the UK, who was a specialist in cultural dimensions in foreign language education. His lecture created a deep impression on me. I realised that my experience in working in China and then Qatar had a lot to do with culture. Though I was teaching the same language, I found myself using very different approaches to dealing with the students in the classroom. It became clear to me that a PhD study in this area could be as fascinating as the sociolinguistic topic that I had proposed to Peter Trudgil at Essex.

Two other factors enhanced my decision to work in this area of research. From a former PhD student of Mike Byram, I found out that he was not only an intellectual heavyweight in cultural studies in foreign language education, but also a supervisor who was very approachable, amiable and pleasant to work with. It also happened that Durham was promoting its international profile overseas and allowed part-time study at discounted fees. After some reading in this area of research, I got in touch with Mike Byram and made a research proposal for my PhD study. Through further correspondence with him and the university, I was formally admitted as a part-time PhD student in 1994 with him as my supervisor. My research focused on cultural dimensions in English language education in China, the context I was most familiar with. Because of the Chinese focus of my PhD study, data had to be collected from China. As a full-time employee of the University of Qatar, to do so would mean taking some time off. This was not a financially viable option.

In the following year, I managed to find a job teaching English as a foreign language in a university in Hong Kong, which was clearly a good solution. It was relatively easy to make data collection arrangements in different cities inside China through various connections and to revisit them if necessary, as Hong Kong was close to the site of my research. Thanks to the fact that Durham was running an Education Doctorate (EdD) programme in Hong Kong and Mike Byram was visiting there at least once a year either for teaching or as Director of the EdD programme, he was able to provide supervision face to face in Hong Kong, which saved me the need to visit Durham for this purpose. The PhD study was thus progressing smoothly.

A setback

Life often challenges people with its uncertainty and unexpectedness. On July 1 1997, the ceremony that marked the return of Hong Kong to Chinese sovereignty was watched with interest by people all over the world. At that moment, few people in Hong Kong were aware what consequences the event would have on their lives and careers. Many hoped the event would not lead to drastic changes, as the Basic Law stipulates that Hong Kong could keep its political system for another 50 years. However, there were changes. In language education, for example, mother tongue education was propagated and implemented swiftly, and funds for English language education were cut severely. This turned out to be a disaster for me. My salary was dependent on the English Language Enhancement Fund. Because of the cuts, many teachers like me were facing redundancy. The effects of this on my research and my life should not be difficult to imagine.

Hunting for a new job was depressing and time-consuming. After several unsuccessful applications, I became aware that all tertiary institutions were cautious about recruiting English language instructors in that political atmosphere. I looked elsewhere and fortunately was successful in securing a similar job at the National University of Singapore. Although the set-back was eventually dealt with, the job hunting and the move cost me a substantial amount of time and clearly affected the momentum of my PhD research study.

What made this episode particularly memorable was the fact that language policies could become so politicised that they could hugely affect individuals and the general public. The effect on me as a language educator was immediate and explicit, but the effects on many in Hong Kong society were subtle and surreptitious. Debates on the politically motivated mother tongue education policy, which was most evidenced by the strict control of the number of EMI (English as the medium of instruction) schools, have continued since the handover[6].

A PhD – final destination?

After six years of work on my PhD project, I finally completed the thesis and submitted it in 1999. A successful viva earned me the degree early the following year. On reflection, the whole PhD research study was a battle fought in four different countries which lasted for nine years from the very start of the idea to the finish. It was a hard battle to do the degree while working full-time, but I had no regrets. Academically, it was unquestionable that the journey made me a better researcher and a more knowledgeable person.

The knowledge I had gained was nevertheless rather limited. More important was the fact that, throughout the journey, I knew that my perspectives on the world had been hugely transformed. I no longer viewed language teaching as imparting linguistic know-how to learners or as pure skills training, but as part of a general education and as a socio-political phenomenon. The research journey enabled me to ask complex questions on the relationships between language education and politics, between language and culture, and between language and citizenship, as well as questions on equality in language use and language education. After my PhD journey, I did not feel I had reached a destination but instead felt obliged to go further in my search for answers to complex questions that had been triggered during the PhD journey; I wished to contribute in some way to equity and equality in education.

Having worked in Singapore for four years as a lecturer in English language, I was quite used to work and life in the metropolitan city state. My living conditions and financial situation were all reasonably satisfactory. Now that I had a PhD, more job opportunities in the city and in Hong Kong became accessible to me. Not long after being awarded the degree, I learned of a job opportunity offered by Durham University (where I had done my degree). This job met my research ambitions well, as it involved the teaching and supervision of education doctorate students in such areas as intercultural and international education, bilingualism and bilingual education, and to do further research in language education. It was without doubt an intellectually challenging job that required constant professional development in research and in subject knowledge. I was truly interested.

I applied for the job and eventually got it. I owe a debt of gratitude to my family, who had all become used to international mobility and life changes and were agreeable to the move. Even though we knew we would not be financially as well off in the UK as in Singapore and would again have to adapt culturally and linguistically to a new environment, somehow we all looked forward to another new start. I felt that our two daughters had both become good 'third culture kids' who had spent little time in the places where they were born, had moved with their parents from one place to another, and were ready to embrace new places, people and things as well as transnational values, ideas and beliefs.

Exploring potential

We arrived in the UK in 2002. My work at Durham University differed fundamentally from the work I had done for more than two decades. I no longer taught English language courses, but used the language to teach specialised knowledge in intercultural studies in education and bilingualism and to conduct research and supervision. In addition, I offered modern foreign language teaching theory lectures to PGCE (Postgraduate Certificate in Education) Modern Foreign Languages students annually. The job was both challenging and rewarding. Over the years at Durham, I transformed myself from an EFL instructor of Chinese origin who taught language skills to undergraduate students learning English as a foreign or second language, to an educator who teaches and supervises doctoral level students in English and conducts research and publishes in that language. This transformation had started much earlier than 2002, of course, and had been taking place throughout my career. That year, 2002, was simply the turning point that compelled me to explore my potential as an educator and academic researcher.

By working with colleagues such as Mike Byram, my former PhD supervisor and life-long mentor, I began to explore many concepts and theories relevant to intercultural education and bilingualism, and published in these areas. My topics ranged across citizenship, assessment, bilingualism and bilingual education, comparative education, Confucian versus Socratic cultures of learning, and policy studies. They all occurred as natural additions to my publication list as they were researched and written either in response to my own questions about an educational issue or to students' queries for which I had no answers. However, they did surprise my former colleagues in the ELT field. One comment made by an ELT colleague in Singapore was, 'I can't believe you publish on things like citizenship. That sounds so far away from ELT. You seem to be in a different world now, after just a few years.'

Return to *Hunan Nga Zi*?

Years of teaching and research at Durham constantly made me think of one of the thorniest issues in education, the inequality which exists everywhere in the world. It is a huge issue, of course, that concerns researchers of all disciplines in all countries. Since my empirical research field tends to be in China, I often asked the question as to who suffers the most from inequality in education and, as a language education researcher, whether and how this situation could possibly be improved, at least from the language point of view.

In brainstorming about disadvantaged groups, *Hunan Nga Zi* naturally popped up in my mind. In China today, tens of millions of families migrate from remote and impoverished villages to cities in search of a better life, just as my family did five decades ago. A study of the children of these families and their education would be a meaningful thing to do. However, among all the social and ethnic groups in China, it is a commonplace observation that the 55 indigenous ethnic minority groups comprising more than 100,000,000 individuals have suffered the most from inequality in education.

Because of the nation-wide examination system which favours speakers of the national language, Mandarin Chinese, the home language (L1) of a minority group is usually ignored in schools. Even in cases in which their L1 is used as the medium of instruction in the first few years, most minority pupils are often forced to turn to their L2 (Mandarin Chinese) as early as they can in order to take the national exams in Chinese. If their L2 is inadequately developed, which is the case for most minority pupils, the use of L2 as the medium of learning and teaching is no doubt detrimental to their cognitive development.

Coupled with other unfavourable factors that minority groups usually face, such as harsh geographical and economic conditions, minority pupils either lag far behind their Han majority counterparts or simply drop out of school. Poor primary and secondary school education in turn affects their chances for higher education and life opportunities.

While my interest in researching language provision for children like *Hunan Nga Zi* remained high, my focus shifted to even more disadvantaged ethnic minority groups. As to the question whether and how this situation could possibly be rectified or improved, the answer is even less straightforward than that to the 'who' question. In the last couple of decades when the government's attitude has been relatively favourable, different measures have been taken to improve the situation. For example, 'preferential policies'[7] are adopted by authorities at various levels to allow minority students with lower scores in national college entrance examinations to enter universities. This seems to offer minority students some equality in education, but once they are in the job market, they still face discrimination as they are labelled as low achievers who depend on preferential policies to enter and complete tertiary education. Much research has shown the ineffectiveness of such measures.

Through a wide range of reading and research in the past few years, I saw some possibilities of making a difference to the situation. Theoretically, insights from research in sociolinguistics, psychology and cultural studies[8] are enlightening and revealing. In practice, I observed that, in Europe alone, there are several countries or places in which effective language education policies and practices have brought about some differences to linguistic minority groups. Wales, Ireland and the Basque Country[9] are such examples. As a result of strong promotion of L1, minority groups in these places feel empowered. Thanks to vigorous application of sound research, pupils not only become bi- or multilingual but perform well in other school subjects. Their experience has demonstrated that research-informed language policies and appropriate approaches to language teaching and learning can contribute to the rectification of many issues in minority education.

A dream project

After seven years of challenging but rewarding experiences in Durham, I made another move in 2008 – to Bangor University in North Wales. With its prestigious Research Centre on Bilingualism, funded by the Economic and Social Research Council, Bangor is a leader in research on bilingualism and bilingual education in the UK and in Europe. Drawing upon ideas and insights from this centre and the research-intensive university in its unique bilingual environment, Welsh and English, I initiated and led with a like-minded professor at the Hong Kong Institute of Education the trilingualism and trilingual education research project in China, with the ambitious aim of improving language provision for China's 100,000,000 minority population.

The project is characterised by the following. First, it aims to gain a holistic understanding of language use and language education of the 55 minority groups throughout the country. Most, if not all, research projects carried out in the minority regions in the past have been rather isolated on regional scales. Comparisons between regions and collaborated research are rare. We have gradually developed a national network of researchers in many minority regions throughout the country and this network is still expanding.

Second, as the title of the project suggests, we intend to study the interrelationship of the three languages which minority pupils have to deal with in the 21st century: the minority home language (L1), Mandarin Chinese (L2) and English (L3). Previous research has mostly either dealt with the relationship between L1 and L2, or focused on how minority pupils learn L3. Trilingualism and trilingual education are recent phenomena in the new century.

Third, the project aims to investigate the experience of linguistic groups such as Cantonese who speak a dialect of Chinese which is so distant from Mandarin Chinese in terms of phonology, vocabulary and syntax that there is no mutual intelligibility between them. Much of the experience of these speakers in language use and language education is not too different from that of ethnic minority groups.

Last but not least, as the methodology is informed by recent research findings on trilingualism or multilingualism reported internationally, we aim to investigate the ethnolinguistic vitality of each minority language under study and assess its potential functions in minority education. We believe revitalisation and empowerment of L1 are necessary in most, if not all cases and more use of L1 can facilitate the learning of L2 and L3 and benefit cognitive development in general.

Despite careful planning and research design, carrying out this ambitious project effectively in mostly remote and underdeveloped minority regions is an enormous challenge. However, my intention to make a difference for the disadvantaged groups through language education is unwavering. Although I am not a member of an ethnic minority group, my own experience in growing up in a socially and economically deprived family has always had an effect on the way I look at the world. Now, I feel the knowledge I have gained through all these years of searching and exploration in the academy (the higher education institutions) has equipped me with the necessary skills and intelligence to improve the situation.

Always dream

My personal journey during all these years has certainly been a rocky one. There were times when I was excited and inspired; times when I was perplexed and bewildered; times when I was very proud of myself. There were also times when I doubted my own worth in the academy. On reflection, however, one thing looks certain. One always dreams. Some dreams can come true unexpectedly; some may require real courage, time and effort to realise; some may be simply mirages. There are dreams one quickly forgets and there are dreams one may chase in earnest.

The realisation of my dreams as a teenager from a low-status family to attend a good secondary school and university is the most inexplicable, particularly from today's materialistic point of view. I attribute this mainly to luck. However, life opportunities do indeed depend upon all kinds of factors, with luck being one of them. In a human society, when one is situated in a particular setting and surrounded by unique individuals, something unusual, something inexplicable might happen. Logical analysis may lose its appeal in these cases. However, my chase for higher degrees is more easily explained in psychological and socioeconomic terms. As the old Chinese saying goes, people climb up the hill (social ladders) while water runs down the stream. In hindsight, what remains most incomprehensible, even to myself, is the multifaceted motivation that sometimes drives me to move from an economic and academic comfort zone to new zones that are challenging and uncertain. It seems that it is along the borderlines between luck, reality and dream that I have been roaming all these years.

Notes

1 The Great Leap Forward was an economic and social plan adopted by the Communist Party under Mao Zedong in the late 1950s to rapidly transform China into a modern socialist society through the process of collectivisation, and industrialisation. It ended in disaster, triggering a widespread famine that resulted in the deaths of millions of people, especially in the countryside (see Thaxton, 2008, for a detailed account of the movement and an in-depth study of a rural village's memories of the famine).

2 The phenomenon of 'worker-peasant-soldier' students during the second half of the Cultural Revolution between 1970 and 1976 was unprecedented in every way in the higher educational history of China and perhaps of the world. While the Cultural

Revolution was still under way, many Chinese universities and colleges enrolled a large number of 'worker-peasant-soldier' students through a politically complex recommendation system (Chen, 1999) as the normal university entrance examinations had been abolished. This system ended when the entrance examination system was reinstated in 1977.

3 During those years, even a tape recorder was rare. In terms of human resources, many English teachers in universities were unqualified. Some who taught us had been Russian teachers but had transformed themselves into English teachers after short training (see Fu, 1986; Adamson, 2004 for a history of English language education in China).

4 TOEFL – Test of English as a Foreign Language – is an internationally accepted standard of English that measures the English proficiency of a non-native speaker of English. It used to be, and still is, seen as the entry requirement for American universities in the 1980s and 1990s in China. Many Chinese students in the 1980s were very familiar with TOEFL, but not with IELTS.

5 'Face' is an extremely important sociological and psychological concept for the Chinese (Bond, 1991; Ho, 1976). It is often used to refer to the respectability and esteem that a person can claim in society. It is not only important for an individual but also linked with his/her family. So, Chinese people often invest emotionally, socially and economically in face. Face can be lost, so constant maintenance and enhancement is necessary.

6 Lin and Man (2009) document this debate in detail in Chapters 4 and 5 of their monograph. The mother tongue education policy was, they argue, part of the political agenda which has been hidden behind the official discourse of pedagogical benefits.

7 'Preferential policy' is one of the most debated topics in the literature on minority education. This policy is made at the national as well as regional or provincial levels to allow minority students with lower university entrance exam marks than their Han counterparts to enter tertiary institutions. Such a policy, many scholars argue, looks positive but actually has a negative effect on minority students. For example, because of the 'labelling effects', minority students are seen as inferior to their majority counterparts on campuses and are not fairly treated in the job market.

8 In the growing volume of literature, I find extremely insightful and inspiring works such as Bialystok (2001), Cummins (1996, 2000) Edwards (1985) and Pavlenko and Blackledge (2004).

9 There is a huge body of literature on bilingual/multilingual education in these parts of the world. Some recent volumes include Cenoz (2009), Garcia (2009), O'Riagain (1997) and Williams (2003). They are all very informative and inspiring to my research.

4

An undergraduate student in Liverpool: a woman's struggle

Xiang Li

My name is Xiang Li, and I was born in Shenzhen in the spring of 1988. Because my sign of the zodiac was the dragon, my parents named me *Xiang*, which means 'dragon soaring in the sky', in the hope that one day their daughter would reach the summit of success. This is the story of my personal learning journey across two continents, chasing my dream to become an independent learner through studying abroad. There have been critical turning points in this journey so far: I have witnessed passion and frustration, and love and disappointment; most importantly, these ups and downs and twists and turns have enriched my personal growth.

My story begins with my birthplace, which has benefited from the policy of reform and opening-up to the outside world. My parents numbered among the few fortunate university graduates to be assigned work in a tiny village called Shenzhen after the period of Cultural Revolution. From its humble origins of mostly rice paddies and ramshackle factories, Shenzhen now has a population of about nine million (Shenzhen Government Online, 2009), a glinting skyline of glass-encased skyscrapers, and a tigerish economy rivalling that of its neighbour, Hong Kong. Shenzhen was one of the first economic zones created by the Chinese Communist Party in the late 1970s. But Shenzhen is more than a boom town. It is a society of modern-day nomads, filled with Chinese from all parts of the country and many foreigners, attracted by the business opportunities. It is a city in the vanguard of reform and economic liberalisation. It places great emphasis on learning English and holistic and integrative education, and is hugely influenced by its distinct media, policies and demographics.

Throughout my childhood I experienced the rapid development of Shenzhen and the city's special attitudes towards the western world. When I was about 5 years old, my parents encouraged me to learn English and helped me develop an interest in sports and the arts. I was highly motivated to learn English and aware of the importance of being fluent. At the age of 7, I was enrolled in a reputable primary school and I was very enthusiastic and positive throughout the six years of an amazing learning journey as I won many awards and medals in sports and national Olympic maths competitions.

A frustrating and bumpy road

However, the happy learning journey took a twist when I was selected to join an experimental class for gifted children, in which three years of junior middle school courses were condensed into two years. Joining the class was a tough decision and it profoundly affected my future journey. Compared to my peers, I had to cope with a far more intensive learning environment and had to push myself towards many seemingly unachievable goals. My class was full of science geniuses (or geeks) who did not need to study hard and were mostly self-taught. Not surprisingly, I struggled to maintain an average position in my class. Looking back, these two years in a way distorted my early teens and left a depressive imprint on my memory. I was deprived of much leisure and freedom and this resulted in gloomy years at middle school and high school later on. Whilst some of my peers enjoyed their early adolescence and teenage rebellion, I felt a touch of envy that I had missed out on an essential part of my teenage experience.

During that time, English was my strongest subject and I learned it comparatively effortlessly as fundamentally it required only good rote memorisation to obtain high marks. At that stage, I was more of a dependent learner, spoon-fed by my teachers. However, there were signs that I was breaking away from this learning pattern as I gradually got to grips with western culture, such as pop music and American soaps. Although

I was again admitted to a key high school, I still lacked confidence as I did not turn out to be as outstanding a student as I had been in my glorious primary school years. The three years were more of a test of my psychological strength than my intelligence, as the National College Entrance Examination (NCEE) is seen as the 'most pressure packed examination in the world' (Siegel, 2007). It is an annual examination taken by students in their last year of high school, and is virtually a compulsory requirement for college admission, the equivalent of A-level exams and SATs in the UK and USA. Therefore the exam is of utmost importance to almost ten million high school students nationwide as it is often the main determinant factor in getting into a famous university in mainland China (Xinhua, 2010). Although I performed quite well in some mock tests, I was constantly stressed because I did not make the elite list in my school. From then on, I was aware that I lacked the psychological maturity to deal with pressure. Not surprisingly, my performance suffered and my class ranking fluctuated dramatically.

Meanwhile, some of my classmates decided to go abroad for their higher education. While I had always been jealous of such people, I had never thought seriously about doing the same, as my parents did not show any support. In retrospect, I think I was too blinded by the pressure to join the top ranks of students and did not position myself for the long term. I did not have a very clear self-image. My mind was too preoccupied with rankings and scores, and in most cases, my thoughts went into a cul-de-sac. Like most high school graduates, I continued higher education in China, setting aside any dreams of studying abroad.

My learning experiences in a Chinese university

In 2006, due to a deterioration in my academic performance, I ended up in a top university in Guangzhou province instead of my first choice, which was the University of Hong Kong. Initially, I felt like a stray bird, living in the shadow of the NCEE, dissatisfied with the courses I was taking. English was taught in the same way as in the 1970s. It was still a heavily test-oriented system, and a few tutors and teaching assistants were still postgraduate students themselves. Many students expressed frustration at the limited choices in changing courses, and the relative lack of freedom in transferring to other universities or faculties, compared to universities in western countries.

As it was, I found other ways to find fulfilment in my student life. Despite less than impressive achievements in academic study, I threw myself into a diverse range of extracurricular activities: participating in volunteer programmes such as poverty alleviation and private tutoring for the poor, filming and editing news programmes on campus as a camera operator and journalist, and similar projects. Having a tight schedule every day smoothed out some of the disappointments of higher education. Since I was discontented with the quality of teaching and learning in class, I started exploring other ways to enhance my intensive and extensive learning. I broadened my horizons and developed interests in other disciplines apart from English. I sat in on courses in other faculties such as economics and management as well as lectures for junior students of my own faculty. The knowledge I gained in this way during these two years proved to be very helpful in my later study in Liverpool. They paved the way for some challenging subjects I took at university in the UK and enabled me have a better understanding of those issues.

As English was my main subject, I continued to put great effort into it, but from a multidimensional approach rather than learning it as a discrete subject. I identified reliable resources for learning apart from sticking to the Oxford Dictionary and core textbooks. I found effective ways of learning through the internet, media and computer games in English. It was very important that these were authentic English sources that were not influenced by Chinglish. I was encouraged by one of my tutors to read books and magazines, such as *Reader's Digest* and *National Geographic*, in the original. However, my English test scores were seldom satisfactory and rather average, an outcome which really hit home to me, and I wondered whether my ability was truly reflected through these so-called exams. Sometimes I cast doubts on the answers given by the teacher or authority figure. Even worse, the results did not necessarily correlate to the time and effort I spent on my study.

In my first year, I gradually became a regular visitor to the BBC China website, which provided a well-rounded platform for people to learn English and culture from radio programmes and texts. This was the first time I realised that the English I had learned was neither purely British nor American English, and I undertook to eradicate the American influence in my English. That website has been undeniably very beneficial to me, serving as a cushion to reduce the coming culture shock by familiarising me with life in Britain.

Living with other university students in halls of residence also helped me to know more about their different lives. One of my flatmates was constantly finding part-time jobs and working all hours to make ends meet. Her restless spirit taught me a lesson about what people could achieve even in unfavourable conditions (coming from a poor and dysfunctional family). She was the dormitory head, in charge of maintenance and organising regular clean-ups. She told me off several times and I initially paid no attention to what she said but later apologised and turned over a new leaf. Thus I learned the reality of social co-existence from flatmates and classmates who were from different backgrounds; life is not as easy as it appears on the outside. I came to realise that I had taken many things for granted. In the volunteering programme, I witnessed and experienced poor children's lives and education in desolate mountainous areas. My team helped out in delivering teaching assistance in one of the villages in Jinggang Mountain, a place of great revolutionary history but one that was yet to shake off the yoke of poverty. Their craving for knowledge and arduous efforts in the mountains made me feel ashamed of myself.

At the end of my sophomore year, a new opportunity for change in my life presented itself. In 2008, my faculty introduced a 2+2 collaboration programme with a tertiary institute in the north west of England which had recently obtained university status. In this programme, students can go on exchange to the UK for their third and fourth years' study. This time, without too much hesitation, my parents and I decided that I would take part in this exchange programme because I could not afford to miss this wonderful chance to free myself from the Chinese education system. My learning journey again took a twist, which allowed me to rediscover myself through studying and living abroad.

Rising to the challenges of studying in the UK

Although this was not the first time I had been abroad – I had been to Britain and Australia as a tourist during my freshman and sophomore holidays – studying and living in the UK still constituted a great challenge to me, both physically and mentally. I took the initiative to learn to adapt to the host country linguistically, socially and culturally.

Language development

My first challenge was the language barrier, which was more formidable than I had expected. The moment I landed at Manchester International Airport, I was bombarded with different varieties of English, of which I could hardly make head nor tail. Even paying bills was difficult, as I did not know the word 'quid' meant pound. But this was only the beginning of the adventure. The more people I got to know as time went by, the more I realised how diverse English was in terms of its varieties and dialects. Liverpool English epitomises a typical dialect: Scouse, with its accent and intonation, initially sounded like gobbledegook to all of us from China. Even some English students admitted having difficulty in understanding it. I was surprised by the fact that although we had learned English for many years and had done thousands of tests, we still had a long way to go in adapting to regional life in an English-speaking country.

Another aspect I discovered was that British English is, to a certain degree, profoundly different from American English in terms of phonology, vocabulary and even grammar. The more I interacted with the locals, the more I found that I had been strongly influenced by American English, probably due to the fact that on a global scale, American TV programmes have gradually become more influential than others. I encountered some difficulty in understanding even the most basic conversations ('crisps' versus 'chips'; 'subway' versus 'underground'). For example, the word 'college' has different meanings in American English and British English. I was confused when people asked me if I had previously attended a college. I figured out that, whilst college is more or less synonymous with university in an American context, it refers to any institution for specialised education after the age of 16 in British English. There were quite a few words which I knew them for but caused misunderstanding when I used them in Britain. Besides, British English encompasses a much greater use of vocabulary and slang, which can be very different from the American and also less familiar to Chinese students: eg 'cheers' is a common word for thank you, 'tara' for goodbye, 'knackered' for tired, 'bloke' and 'lad' for man, and 'skint' for broke.

Additionally, I struggled with the pragmatic aspect of English, which is related to one's cultural and psychological mindset. I found myself hesitating over how to reply to questions such as 'How are you?', 'You all right?' or taking the initiative to greet people in this way.

Although I had met a few international students back in my university in China, I never got a chance to talk to them. It was in this UK university that I was able to communicate with students from across the globe. The English language was instrumental in cultural exchanges: its power as a *lingua franca* that connects people from different places was evident, and reflected in cross-cultural communications. Whilst I was amazed at the power and importance of English, I also experienced other varieties of English (Bolton and Kachru, 2006), including Indian English, Korean English and African English. Through our interactions, I found that these international students and exchange students usually had a better grip on English than I did especially in terms of speaking, and they were very confident when expressing their opinions. Although Chinese students may have a wider vocabulary and better accent than some other international students, we were still not as fluent and less comfortable in speaking out loud. This further spurred me on to progress in learning English.

I gradually become a very loyal fan of the BBC. Every day, my schedule began with the Radio 1 UK chart show in the morning and news programmes and soaps on iPlayer at night. The introduction of the iPlayer allowed residents in the UK to catch up on the last seven days of BBC TV and radio and replay the programmes as many times as they wanted within a certain period (BBC, 2007). Apart from convenience, iPlayer is also powerful and attractive to me as most programmes have subtitles, which can help me better understand the content, improve my listening and enlarge my vocabulary on the one hand and learn about current issues and social phenomena on the other.

Whilst watching these programmes, I could see that my motherland China has been the target of criticism and its actions and policies with regard to human rights and Tibet, for instance, were often interpreted rather negatively. Although British soaps, sitcoms and dramas are not as popular as their American counterparts, it does not necessarily mean that they are any less intriguing. In fact, they can be more twisted and less predictable than some of the American programmes in which justice and the hero always wins. For example, the teenage drama 'Skins' (a realistic portrait of modern rebellious teenagers) controversially explores issues including dysfunctional families, homosexuality, sex, drugs and mental illness. Many reality shows associated with America, such as 'X Factor' and 'America's Got Talent', actually originated in Britain. Watching such programmes, I not only enjoyed the funny, peculiar and astounding acts, but also learned ways of giving comments and opinions. Shows such as 'The Jeremy Kyle Show', and 'The World's Strictest Parents' revealed the severity of family disputes, domestic violence, and the behaviour of feral teenagers. Society is never as perfect as it might appear to be.

Coping with different learning styles

The exchange programme was not very flexible since several restrictions were imposed on it. At first I was not very satisfied, as participants were required to take at least two modules out of four in the subject area of English, which did not appeal to me in the slightest. However, as time went on, I gradually developed an interest in sociolinguistics and psycholinguistics. I was very keen on the language acquisition theory proposed by Chomsky, the fascinating and controversial universal grammar (UG) hypothesis (1968). In one of my projects, I attempted to critically evaluate UG in the Chinese language context. My tutors gave me a lot of support and encouraged me to be the top student in the English class – my grades greatly exceeded those of the British students. I was also very interested in bilingualism in the social context, issues like language shift and maintenance, and culture and identity, which are relevant to the British-born Chinese generation (with whom I had some contact facilitated by the fact that I myself had lived and studied in two continents).

The learning style of higher education in the UK is very different from that in China, at least in my experience. In UK universities, tutors conduct lectures and seminars: lectures give a general view of the topic whilst seminars are more student-led group discussions. Besides, each week tutors will set aside a surgery hour (usually there is a sheet posted on the office door where students can sign up for slots) in which students can discuss their questions and seek help from tutors. Before attending lectures and seminars, students are required to do considerable reading; prior to writing essays and projects, they often need to read extensively to locate a specific topic and form a critical view on the subject.

Back in China, I had seldom visited the library for academic books or a database – simple online research or a Google search would be sufficient for my essays. I only had traditional lectures which were predominately teacher-orientated and the concept of setting aside an office hour for students was rarely found. Students usually remained very distant from professors or tutors.

This was the first time I realised that the tutor-student relationship can be so pivotal in students' study. I was encouraged to make good use of the office hour by my tutors, and they were very helpful in providing me with relevant guidelines and resources. Conversation in surgery hours does not have to be serious all the time; it could be relaxed and funny. In the UK, unlike China, tutors and students may address each other by their first name or as 'mate', 'pal', and in some cases even 'darling' or 'love', which seems to place teachers and students in a more intimate relationship. However, tutors were not giving students everything on a plate; most importantly, they acted as a mentor providing students with a general direction, and encouraging them to conduct independent projects with creativity and originality.

The library resources were crucial in developing one's academic research ability. From introductory sessions, seminars and expert librarians, I grasped some basic researching skills and learned about the classification of databases. Sometimes, due to the limited resources in the library and database subscriptions, I asked friends from other universities to access online journals and help my research. I made good use of my network of friends to borrow books from other universities in Liverpool. I found that resources from the central library in the city could be of tremendous assistance in my study. On several occasions I even sent emails to scholars for copies of their works to help my research. To my surprise, a few of them responded to my requests and were willing to help me.

However, neither tutors nor the library could directly help students with their academic writing. In the feedback on my first essay, my tutor commented that despite the fact that it was well-researched, some of the language was 'awkward and weird'. In order to improve my academic writing, I read related academic journals, books and newspapers, and made notes on formal English and the proper writing style. Before submitting my essays, I would go to the writing centre or ask native English speakers to proof-read them for me.

Another distinction between the two learning systems is the emphasis on referencing. In UK universities, casual referencing can be considered as plagiarism and such an accusation can be serious enough to cause a student to be expelled. In stark contrast, the concept of intellectual property and referencing has yet to enter into the mindset of most Chinese university students. They write numerous essays and assignments but are seldom reminded or have the self awareness to give credit to their sources. Plagiarism is common practice and it does not seem to be taken seriously. Students are not well informed about the referencing system until the dissertation submission. In my opinion, knowing the importance and legitimacy of referencing is the first step towards producing an academic essay.

Responding to the social and cultural challenges

As this UK university is relatively small, it has fewer student organisations and associations than my university in China. I joined the women's basketball club as I had always been fond of playing this game. As first it was difficult to fit in as the majority of the squad were Irish and British, as well as a few other Europeans. I felt very neglected – even awkward – as I was the only Asian student, and training involved a lot of jargon which confused me. But I managed to stay positive and my outstanding shooting skills were gradually recognised by the coach and my teammates. After some ice-breaking conversations and good performances, I became more involved in training and matches. Everything went well on court and but I was not keen to go out drinking with them. Because I am allergic to alcohol and disapprove of some aspects of the British lifestyle, I do not like the drinking culture. Then I realised that drinking is part of the social scene, like dining out in China. Initially I experienced a lot of conflict in my mind about whether I should force myself to go out with them, but after attending a few nights out where I witnessed some unacceptable pranks (such as excessive and inappropriate drinking games), I decided that I would only go to fund-raising events and meals to mark special occasions. I learned how to say no and turn down invitations in a polite way.

Because of my good record of training attendance and my frequent assistance in chores and errands for the management group, I was nominated and elected by the team as kit manager at the end of the first year. This was the first time I had genuinely earned trust from British students and I was very grateful to them.

At the end of the second year, I was awarded the certificate of achievement for women's basketball for my continued learning of the English language during training and games. In each session, I learned a couple of new slang words and phrases (even taboo and derogatory words – which revealed another aspect of the English vocabulary) and this provided an opportunity to learn about the degree of offensiveness and pragmatics of swearing. Sometimes my questions embarrassed the British students and some of these became running jokes among us. I realised that I enjoyed learning the language and culture but did not agree with some of its values and practices. For me, learning English has become an instrumental medium for communication and friendship but has not necessarily reflected inner culture assimilation and loss of traditional values. As Hoffman (1990) indicated, it is wrong to assume that English proficiency is linked to greater acculturation. My cultural identity was still maintained as Chinese whilst sometimes positive western elements were incorporated. It was a process of striking a good balance between various cultures and dealing with different values harmoniously. At the end-of-year meal for the basketball squad, the team bought me some gifts as a surprise – a basketball and a bag of wheat noodles, which was a bit of prank as they all knew I was allergic to wheat noodles.

When I came to England, its economy was severely affected by the financial meltdown and credit crunch, making it particularly difficult to get a part-time job, especially for international students. As I wanted to gain some work experience and know more about Britain from different perspectives, I decided to apply for volunteer work at one of the famous charity organisations, Oxfam. Fortunately, I was instantly offered work on a trial basis. This was the first time I had gone through a formal work interview and I could not conceal my excitement.

Working in the shop as a volunteer was not easy. I had to learn everything from scratch, such as steaming clothes and stock management.

Sometimes it was physically as well as mentally demanding as I worked both front of shop and in the backroom. Steaming clothes is not as simple a job as it seems. You need to do up every button before steaming and to use skirt hangers for wide necked clothes in case they fall off. Whilst sorting out heaps of donations, I got to know the household names in fashion, and those of celebrities. I kept a log of the things I learned from every shift. It was a good chance to track my learning about the language and culture from a perspective off campus and with a different set of British people. When it was not so busy, I could often share lovely conversations with colleagues on the shift, most of whom were mature volunteers, retired elder people such as Bill, an old gentleman who always wore his hunting cap and loved word puzzles. I remember our conversation exploring words with the affix of saw. The first one was tenon-saw as he asked the manager for one. Hand saw, fret saw seesaw – he illustrated each saw with a picture. Finally he said he had a 'hand sore' when he had done too much sawing.

The volunteer work also gave me an understanding of the operations flow in a charity shop. I got to know about some campaigns and programmes that Oxfam promoted worldwide: e.g., its fair trade products and gift-aided items aim to improve the welfare of the poor. The knowledge and experience I gained in Oxfam was helpful when I did an NGO case study for one of my business essays. The people-centred capacity building strategy (Eade, 1997) was clearly reflected in this Oxfam charity shop. I felt so fulfilled every time I worked there. I was so delighted when a staff member warmly held my hand and gave me a gentle kiss on the cheek, whispering 'you made a difference in the shop today'. At the end of my volunteer work, a staff member from the book team selected two books on English idioms as a gift for me.

People I met in the UK who have shaped my views of the world

My journey in the UK was greatly influenced by a few key people I met. Unlike some international students who came in a tight-knit group and only stayed with those people, I attempted to be more extroverted, learning to approach different people and as a result I met some truly amazing people that I am now lucky enough to call my friends. They have been good company for me and added colour to my adventure.

Mark

I had never actually talked to black people before and my preconception of them was they were very poor and not well-educated. However, my encounter with a black gentleman called Mark has dramatically changed my perception. Mark stopped me outside a lecture hall one day (although my intuition strongly told me to step back) and we started our friendship with a conversation. At the age of 62, he was a returning student studying sociology and politics and was full of energy. (In UK universities, mature students form a significant proportion of the full-time student population.) To my surprise, he spoke Standard English and had a profound knowledge of history and politics, and even knew more about Chinese history than I did. He was writing a book, *The Birth of Modern Racism in Britain*, which is very insightful and interesting, with abundant examples and sophisticated language. Fist-bumping was the way we greeted and bid farewell to each other. He told me it was a trendy way of greeting originally used by black athletes to show their solidarity against racism.

Despite his economic disadvantage, he displayed his principle of altruism. He offered me his phone number when we first met and told me to feel free to contact him if I had any problems or questions to ask. I was a bit shocked at first, and thought it was just out of courtesy that he had given me the number. As promised, he was delighted to read my essays and discussed issues within and beyond them. Unlike the sessions provided in the writing centre, which were always in a rush, and where the peer tutor could not be bothered with proof reading and often turned out to be inexperienced and not very knowledgeable, Mark could give me specific instructions in terms of language and content. He often added notes commenting on my examples and related them to other historical events or everyday life. He became a big brother to me, and he was more like a personal tutor in helping me to adapt to the British language and culture (the car boot sale; world politics; the general election; the decadence of western society and the church; the assassination theory of Diana's death; British views of China's development).

However, in spite of his courage and altruism, he had several arguments with some of the university tutors and students. At the beginning of the second year, he was expelled from the university and forbidden to set foot on the premises. His defiance against the university and establishment sometimes made me feel confused: I could not understand his stubbornness, which often turned out to be futile, but I did appreciate his spirit.

In spite of what had happened, I kept in touch with him, asking him to proof-read my essays and inviting him to my friend's house for tea. I could tell he was moved and delighted when my compatriots packed take-away boxes of Chinese cuisine for him during the Spring Festival – he could not celebrate it with us because it was prohibited. After his expulsion from the university, he did not give up his pursuit of higher education even though he was turned down by other universities.

A business tutor

During the two years of the exchange, one of my business tutors, in particular, had a great influence on my study. She was aware of the Chinese student's limited understanding of slang so she explained every slang expression she used in lectures. She nicknamed herself Ms Kitten, often made fun of herself and used a lot of humour in class. Later on, I found out she was a lesbian. She often openly used herself as an example to illustrate unfair treatment and discrimination, blending in some sarcastic humour. I had never had any contact with homosexuals before, and in China in the 1990s homosexuals were regarded as peculiar – even as suffering from a mental disorder (Xinhua, 2005). But the more I got to know her, the more I found she had a great personality and I developed a very good relationship with her. She invested huge effort in getting international students involved with British students in seminar activities by issuing numbered cards so that, in each seminar, we would work with different students and familiarise ourselves with different cultures and opinions. In office surgery, we discussed many things, from essays and study, to personal issues such as how to get along with people and cope with a new culture.

Margaret

Gradually, I found that the mature students were more approachable and more willing to answer my idiotic questions, which were ignored by my peers. I developed a deep friendship with a note-taker, Margaret (who sat next to her blind client in order to read out notes during the lecture). Each time I came to the seminar I brought some questions with me and discussed some political or culturally sensitive issues with her and I enjoyed this. Margaret encouraged me to watch musicals and pantomimes such as 'Phantom of the Opera' and 'Peter Pan'. I learned how to appreciate and further develop my interest in theatre. Stage productions were very sophisticated in integrating technology into the music. I found watching live theatre very enjoyable as I could fully immerse myself in the show and the interaction between the characters and the audience. The music was not pre-recorded but played by an orchestra. Whilst talking to Margaret, I learned that UK universities had quite a few disabled students, which was rare in China. The university supported them in their academic study and day-to-day living. Disabled-friendly services and equipment are widely available in public facilities such as libraries, museums and transportation. To my mind, disabled students were given more opportunities to study and live in a caring environment than in China. Society as whole gives more support and care, which has been reflected in the theme of 2012 Olympic Games.

Anne

I had a good friendship with Anne, a British-born Chinese classmate from my linguistic module whose family originated from Hong Kong. We discussed a lot of interesting topics related to language and cultural identity issues, and found much similarity in our experiences. I was amazed by her Scouse English and her tolerant attitude towards both cultures (she admitted she had been westernised in many ways but still retained some crucial oriental values such as appreciating food culture, and practising diligence and thrift). Her parents had been immigrants from Hong Kong in the 1970s, and she expressed her doubts and confusion about the generation gap between her parents and herself. Her parents were, in her opinion, still very traditionally Chinese and not well integrated into mainstream society. They made unreasonable demands on her, such as insisting that her boyfriends should be of Chinese origin and not allowing her to go out clubbing and drinking. She told me she had experienced culture shock when she returned to Hong Kong a few years ago. Whilst nicknamed 'little Anne' by her British peers, she was regarded as fat and lazy by her Hong Kong relatives.

During our conversations, we communicated in both English and Cantonese, and Anne tended to switch to English in most cases. She admitted it was a shame she was not good at Cantonese because she only used it when talking to her parents. Similar experiences with other British-born Chinese told me that the second generation of Chinese immigrants had some difficulty in preserving their heritage language.

Conclusion

During my stay in England, I not only improved my English proficiency but also broadened my horizons and world view as I attempted to do many things for the first time in my life. I adopted a liberal, flexible attitude toward the language and various cultures, embracing positive elements whilst rejecting inappropriate values. Mingling with different people and enjoying real multiculturalism in Britain was good fun. I had my own pace of integration and acculturation. In the second year, I was introduced to stand-up comedy by a British friend called Andrew. We watched episodes from 'Mock the Week' and 'QI'. While he explained some political vocabulary to me, I learned to appreciate outrageous British satire and hilarious humour.

During my academic study, I realised the differences between China and the UK in higher education, and learned to adapt to the UK system, with its emphasis on being an independent learner. I wrote my dissertation in instant messaging on the topic of code-switching in Chinese university students, and it was rated as one of the excellent theses in my faculty. From being an average student in China, I became a top student at the UK university, being awarded a first class degree and impressing my tutors and fellow students. All of this helped me to regain my long lost confidence, and enabled me to emerge from the shadow of depression and frustration. I learned like a child because children are most effective in language learning (Lenneberg, 1967). As my age was way beyond the critical period for second language acquisition, I needed more self awareness and external stimulus to improve the learning process. Children are like sponges; they absorb massive amounts of information from sources all around them and easily soak up everything (Fisher, 2000: 276). I immersed myself in the English language environment to the maximum in various ways. I kept a learning diary, jotting down every insight I gained, keeping track of my time and reminding myself of my experiences in the UK. In retrospect, my journey is not as glorious or flashy as other people's, but, even when I was at an all time low, there was always a way out and I just needed to pick myself up and be ready for the challenge.

At the end of my UK learning journey, I planned to apply for a master's degree in applied linguistics and education in several UK universities. However, shortly before my graduation, I was offered a post in a state-owned enterprise branch in Hong Kong. I strongly believe these two years in Britain will greatly benefit me in my future journey, and I will treasure the memory for the rest of my life.

5

An Uyghur linguist at an English university: intercultural encounters

Mamtimyn Sunuodula

This chapter focuses on my personal journey of growing up as a boy in a remote part of north western China. I was constantly exposed to unfamiliar cultural, linguistic and social environments after I left school for university at the age of 16 in pursuit of better educational opportunities, cognitive and intellectual fulfilment, and ideals and dreams of freedom and better life. I want to demonstrate how that journey has, in Norton's words (1997), 'transformed' my understanding of my relationship with the world and has continually changed my possibilities for the future. It begins with a childhood that was quite different from the one experienced by most of my contemporaries in the rest of China and by generations who grew up in the same place just a few years later. It then charts one of the most important stages of my life – when I was at university.

I studied psychology just as the subject was being rehabilitated in China, after being banned for many years as 'fake' science by the Communist authorities and was systematically exposed to Western thought for the first time, partly as a result of it. I had to negotiate living and studying with Han students from across China in a predominantly Han linguistic, cultural and social environment, and overcome the linguistic barriers to learning the subject.

It was a time when China had just started implementing policies to open up to the outside world, and economic reforms brought unparalleled changes that formed the basis of the current prosperity of most Chinese citizens. My simple and secure childhood experience growing up in a predominantly Uyghur linguistic and cultural environment, my struggles to overcome linguistic, cultural and social barriers and isolation while at university, my exposure to Western ideas, and the great changes that took place in the whole of China during that period all had a profound effect on the way I saw myself; they created a fertile ground for my growing interest and motivation to explore the world beyond the borders of China and the possibilities for the future.

I describe how I have been constantly constructing and reconstructing the dreams and worldviews I had in China by dynamically adjusting and re-adjusting to my environment and, at the same time, positively influencing, it since my arrival in the UK nearly twenty years ago. I conclude by suggesting that my whole life experience is a mirror of my belief that, although people from different cultural, linguistic, social and ethnic backgrounds are inevitably situated differently in a stratified world and engaged in a dynamic power relationship, as described by Gramsci (1991), there are no boundaries that cannot be overcome. Dreams can be realised through constantly adapting to the new environment, as well as positively influencing it by active learning, participation and, in the process, creating new communities of practice.

Early childhood and the era of the Cultural Revolution
I was born to an Uyghur family in Kashgar, in the far north-western Xinjiang Uyghur Autonomous Region of China at the height of the Cultural Revolution[1]. Xinjiang lies at the heart of the Eurasian continent and had been the centre of trade and cross cultural exchanges between Europe and Asia for many centuries before the dominance of maritime trade. It was an important hub along the famed Silk Road which transported goods, ideas, and religions as well as languages and cultures, among many other things.

Today , Xinjiang Uyghur Autonomous Region occupies one sixth of the total land mass of the People's Republic of China and shares borders with Russia, Kazakhstan, Kyrgyzstan, Tajikistan, Pakistan, Afghanistan, India and Mongolia. It has a complex mixture of ethnic composition and great potential for international exposure, both in sociocultural terms and in economic activities. It was home to almost 21 million people by the end of 2007. The largest ethnic group in Xinjiang are the Uyghurs with a population of some nine million, closely followed by China's dominant Han ethnic group, whose population in the region has increased from less than 7 per cent to over 40 per cent in the last half century (Chinese Academy of Social Sciences, 1994:39-40).

The Uyghurs are a Turkic speaking people who are indigenous to the region and form the absolute majority in the area where I was born and grew up. We spoke the Uyghur language at home, socially and at school, where we were taught in Uyghur much of the time. We had a few Han neighbours whose children were fluent Uyghur and Mandarin Chinese bilinguals, but they went to a separate school from Uyghurs where they were taught in their mother tongue. As children, we often played and socialised together as we grew up. The Han parents were mostly privileged Communist Party officials, factory managers and technical workers. In contrast, most Uyghur parents were either manual labourers or lower level administrators.

The factory provided housing for Uyghur and Han ethnic groups, separated by a children's playground where some vicious dogs roamed around attacking and terrorising children from both groups from time to time. The houses were owned by the factory and any private property was forbidden, other than the household items inside people's homes; it was seen as the seeds of capitalist inclinations. People were not allowed to plant vegetables or any other crops to supplement the food ration that they received from the state. Any form of trading by private individuals was strictly forbidden and most household goods were in short supply. The few state-owned shops that existed were responsible for selling and distributing all the daily necessities and everyone envied the shop keepers, the people who worked at the ration distribution centres and at the butcheries. People competed to be friends with them so they could get the fattest bit of the meat or the cut with less bone.

Everyone in a household had a small ration of cooking oil (half a litre per adult and quarter of a litre per child), corn and wheat flour (80% corn and 20% wheat) per month as well as a meat ration. Every family went to the sole flour and cooking oil distribution centre in a town of

20,000 families at the beginning of each month and fought their way to the distribution counter to get their ration first, as very often the centre ran out of stock and families who were late had to wait extra days to get their ration. Most families would have finished their rations by the end of the previous month and they faced starvation if they did not get their ration at the beginning of the month. It was often a chaotic scene.

The bigger the family the bigger rations. So people had more children and there was no restriction on family size. An average family had around six children – there were six in my family. We had several large sacks for carrying and storing flour and we borrowed factory wheelbarrows and carts to transport it from the ration distribution centre.

People had to show their household registration book to get the rations and only people with city resident status were entitled to this, a privilege denied most people residing outside the town centre. The rural population was classed as peasants and did not receive the same food ration as town dwellers, which meant that they needed to work on the land to produce crops in order to sustain themselves as well as contribute enough grain to the state to meet the quota imposed upon them.

They also had a crop quota for preparations for war with the Soviet Union. Every year a certain proportion of their produce went to meet the state-imposed quota for provisioning the urban dwellers and to contribute to the war preparation reserve. Each peasant earned points for a day's work every day from dawn to dusk throughout the year. At night, they attended political studies or class struggle meetings where they criticised or abused ex-landowners and reactionaries for their past wrongs and praised the Party and its dear leader Chairman Mao. They received a share of the produce at the end of harvest season, depending on the points they had earned.

Many peasants were indebted to their communes because they ate more than their entitlement, and the commune officials went to their houses to confiscate whatever valuables they had. The debt accumulated year after year for many families and at the end it became so large that it was impossible for them to pay it off in full in their life time. They lost all their belongings and the only thing their children inherited from them was their debt to the commune. It was very difficult for many of my classmates at the primary school as they came from these impoverished families.

As one of the six children of a junior factory manager, I could count myself as more fortunate than the children from peasant families at school. Although I hated eating bread made from corn flour and the corn flour porridge we ate in the mornings for breakfast every day, at least it was guaranteed through the ration system and we did not have to suffer from starvation as the peasant children did. My father's priority always seemed to be to ensure that we had enough to eat. Most of our clothes were sewn by my mother out of the trimmings of the thin cotton cloth used for wrapping the processed cotton in the factory. She worked in a shop selling cooked sheep organs, where most customers were peasants who came to the factory to sell their cotton produce. My mother used to treat us to one or two sheep knuckles from time to time on special occasions, such as festivals and birthdays.

The factory had a large allotment which provided the factory workers with fresh fruit and vegetables through the summer; it owned several hundred sheep, pigs and cows which provided additional meat products for the workers. All factory workers had to spend several days a year working in the allotment in planting and harvest seasons. Most children accompanied their parents to the allotment from a very young age and consciously or unconsciously learned the art of agriculture, as well as enjoying delicious fresh fruit during the harvest season. For us children, it was one of the most exciting events in the year, as the factory provided boiled meat soup and other unobtainable foodstuffs.

Part of my father's responsibility in the factory was to manage the allotment and the livestock animals, and I sometimes took advantage of this and was chosen by the allotment caretaker to pick the vegetables when they were ready. I was able to eat as much fruit and vegetables (such as tomatoes and cucumbers) as I could while picking, which was why all children were so keen to help. The produce was distributed to the workers in equal measures. The factory was located on the edge of the town and close to the surrounding agricultural area.

Most Uyghur workers did not know or had a very basic competence in Mandarin; the Han managers knew very little Uyghur. Communication was conducted between the two groups at a very basic level on a daily basis and the factory employed a translator who translated at class struggles and other meetings between Uygur and Han workers. Only two Uyghur families, the factory deputy manager and the Party leader who lived alongside Han families in the Han block, spoke reasonable Mandarin and their children were sent to a Chinese medium school.

One morning when I was 5 years old, I went out to play with some of my friends. We went to the nearby agricultural land and played hide-and-seek in the wheat fields all day, hiding inside the fully grown wheat crop; we returned home late in the afternoon. On the way home we bumped into some children who told us about a new school in the village. I was so curious about what I heard from them that the next morning I went to the same spot again.

The children from the village took me into their school. It was just one room, with a long tree trunk placed horizontally in the middle of the room that served as a bench for all the children in the class to sit on. The floor was just powdery earth and it was used as an exercise book by the children, who wrote with their fingers as pens. The only paper in the classroom was the teacher's worn out Alphabet book and the only writing implements were some broken pieces of white chalk. The other piece of furniture was a small black wooden board hanging on the front wall. The board was much worn and the black coating on the board had faded badly, so it was not easy for the children to see the teacher's writing.

There were around fifteen children in the room ranging from age 5 to age 15. The children took turns every day to take the blackboard home and dye it with black carbon scraped off the bottom of their family saucepan. Normally, each family had only one large saucepan for cooking all their food and the firewood came from the desert poplar forest nearby. The bottom of the saucepan blackened during cooking. I had to ask for my mother's help to turn the saucepan upside down so that I could scrape off the carbon with a knife into a mixing bowl and mix it with water. Then I painted the blackboard with the mixture. The child on duty had to go into school very early and get everything ready before the teacher arrived.

The teacher spoke only Uyghur and did not know any Mandarin, but the lesson contents were translated from Mandarin into Uyghur and we learned revolutionary stories of Communist Party leaders and revolutionary slogans, such as 'Long Live Chairman Mao' and 'Down with the landlords and capitalist class'. We practised copying these words on the floor with our fingers as the teacher wrote them on the blackboard, and each of us was called out to the front to write them again on the blackboard as a test at the end of each lesson. A few months later, we discovered that many of our classmates had exceeded the teacher in terms of writing skill. The teacher was just copying the content of the textbook when he wrote on the blackboard. He spent considerable time reading the students' writing and confirming whether or not their answers were correct. It was obvious that he himself was just literate enough to teach us at a very basic level.

I continued with the class for a year and learned the Uyghur alphabet, which was based on the Pinyin system, a romanisation scheme adopted by the Chinese Communist Party government to help learners pronounce Chinese characters. I must have told my parents about the school but they did not seem to have taken any notice. It was not in any sense a formal education and we spent at least half the school time playing outside in the fields. I enjoyed most of it.

My primary education and the death of Chairman Mao

It was a hot summer's day when one of my friends from the neighbourhood came to our house and told me to go and hide. I asked the reason for this and he said that teachers from the town primary school were coming to the neighbourhood to take children away. I followed him to hide in an underground tunnel originally intended for the seemingly inevitable war with the Soviet imperialist enemy. After about an hour or so, I got rather bored in the tunnel and decided to go out and see what was happening. I saw two female teachers sitting at the edge of the playing field, but could not see any children around. Before I managed to run and disappear, one of the teachers quickly came and grabbed my arm and took me to where they were sitting. They asked for my name, my age and so on, and then they told me that I was still a little too young, but they could accept me for the school starting in the autumn. Then they went to see my parents at home and talked to them about this. Thus, all seemed ready for me to start my formal education.

The new school looked much better than the previous one and was attended by several hundred children. The school buildings looked neat and the playground was not very dusty, as it had regularly been sprayed with water by the school children. The classes ranged from Year 1 to Year 5 and there were several classes in each year group. All the children and teachers were Uyghur, except for one Kazakh teacher who came from the north and taught literature classes for higher grades. There were proper tables and chairs, and a large blackboard on the wall of the classroom, but it was still painted with the saucepan carbon brought to the school by children each day. There was a large portrait of Chairman Mao hanging on the front wall of the classroom and several quotations from him in Uyghur, one of which read 'Study hard and make progress every day', and another, 'You are the early morning sun, hope is bestowed upon you'.

Starting at the new school was an exciting experience for me. We were given proper textbooks, pencils and school bags on the first day of school. I was most excited to see some older children wearing the red Communist Young Pioneer scarf and immediately started dreaming of becoming a pioneer myself. The teacher taught us how to be respectful first to Chairman Mao and the Communist Party, and then to the teachers and the school rules. Every morning, when the teacher entered the classroom we all stood up and solemnly pledged to Chairman Mao the following:

> Our greatest dear leader and greatest teacher Chairman Mao, We will listen to every word you have said and we will carry out everything you direct us to do. You are the Great Father to all children of China. We will forever be loyal to you and to the cause of the Chinese Communist Party.

After the ceremony, the lessons started. We learned about Chairman Mao's life and his works as well as reading and writing in the Uyghur alphabet. We memorised popular quotations from Chairman Mao and his closest comrades. One such quotation, which I have never forgotten, was from Lin Biao, which said 'Read Chairman Mao's books, follow Chairman Mao's words, and do as directed by Chairman Mao.' We learned to sing revolutionary songs, such as 'East is Red', 'Sailing at Sea, We Rely on the Helmsman', the 'Red Guard Song' and many more, although we hardly understood their meaning. Some pupils wore Chairman Mao badges on their chests. Influenced by the revolutionary propaganda and revolutionary atmosphere, most of the children wanted to be People's Liberation Army soldiers when they grew up.

The teacher read us stories about revolutionary heroes, such as Lei Feng, Dong Cunrui and Huang Jiguang, which left a deep impression on me. As a child, I was particularly moved and influenced by the story of Lei Feng, who was ready to give up everything for the people, the Party and the country. Under this influence, I believed that if everybody was ready to give up or share whatever they had, there would be enough of everything in the world and there would be no hardship or suffering. Not only did I share Lei Feng's belief, but I tried to act on it and several times I was held up as a model pupil in the school.

One of the flagship policies for education in China during the Cultural Revolution was the strong emphasis placed on learning from the masses, ie workers and peasants. Many formerly qualified teachers were accused of being influenced by bourgeois ideology and out of touch with reality. They were sent to factories and villages to work and learn from the workers and peasants. Equally, many factory workers and peasants were recruited to the schools to teach children their version of history, about the revolutionary achievements in villages and towns since the Communist Party came to power and how good the people's livelihood had become compared with what life was like before. We spent much of our school time helping in the countryside planting seeds in the spring, harvesting wheat and fruit in summer and picking cotton in autumn.

We were not allowed to criticise the Party or the leadership. Even saying something controversial by accident or a slip of the tongue got people into trouble at school. I vividly remember being severely reprimanded by my father for saying that Chairman Mao looked old, after watching a propaganda film. There were only a few films and they were shown repeatedly all year round in the only cinema in the town. Some were documentaries about the Cultural Revolution and others were feature films about the heroism of the Chinese Communist Party during the long civil war and the war against Japan in the first half of the 20th century. The only other forms of entertainment we had were the revolutionary songs and stories broadcast by the County People's Broadcasting Station via the loudspeakers scattered across the town.

I was studying in Year 4 of the primary school when we heard that Chairman Mao had died. No one dared to say the word 'died' for several days after his death, even after the news was widely broadcast on the loudspeakers. Most people, regardless of their ethnicity, duly dressed in black clothes or wore a black arm band and an artificial white funeral peony on their chest. A mass funeral ceremony was held in the school sports field where many people cried, wailed and even fainted. I did not understand, at the time, what it meant and what the future held.

Some weeks later, it was announced that Chairman Hua Guofeng had been chosen as the successor to Chairman Mao, and the 'Gang of Four' (a group that had seized political control of China and were responsible for some of the excesses of the Cultural Revolution) had dramatically fallen from grace. The school, the town and the whole country organised street marches and demonstrations for several days in celebration.

Chairman Hua did not stay in power for very long. He was soon pushed aside by internal factional fighting within the Party for his intransigent and dogmatic stance on fundamental policies. The liberal factions prevailed and started relaxing the extreme leftist policies. The first visible effects were that people started trading their goods and products more openly in the streets in the town and the peasants who were indebted to the state were released from their debts. This was soon followed by the introduction of a private land leasing scheme, which was the cornerstone of the new economic reform policy. These changes had a dramatic effect on people and their way of life. Agricultural products became plentiful in the markets and dozens of new shops and market stalls opened, selling daily necessities. There was a real optimism in every walk of life and the new policies seemed to have stimulated most people's imagination, creativity and motivation. We no longer had to eat only corn flour bread and porridge every day and for many people in the countryside it was the first time that they had enough food to eat.

My secondary school and a reviving Uyghur identity

I moved to an Uyghur secondary school where I was taught in my mother tongue; all the teachers and students were Uyghurs. We started a six-hour a week compulsory Mandarin course as part of the curriculum. It was the first time that I was taught Chinese characters, though I had learned some colloquial expressions and swear words in my communication with our Han neighbours. The Mandarin teacher was an Uyghur who spoke to us in Uyghur for much of the time. It was very ineffective and we did not learn much about how to write in Chinese characters and even less about speaking in Mandarin. Outside the classroom, we communicated exclusively in our mother tongue, so progress in learning to write and speak in Chinese was extremely slow, despite the various government initiatives and policies, which remained empty words and slogans. This was the case in most Uyghur schools that I knew of at the time.

The Uyghurs remain one of the least literate in Chinese among the many linguistic minorities in China. The Han people who migrated to Xinjiang in large numbers in the past half century appear to be less and less interested in learning Uyghur or the languages of other linguistic minorities in Xinjiang (Table 1; see also Sunuodula and Feng, 2010). These two communities lived and still live almost completely divided lives.

Table 1: Comparison of Chinese (Han) language use among Uyghurs and Tibetans in Tibet (sample study carried out in 1986) Source: Chinese Academy of Social Sciences. Ethnology Research Institute, 1994

	Proficient in Chinese	Some knowledge of Chinese	No knowledge of Chinese	Mother tongue
Tibetans in Tibet	5.7%	9.6%	84.7%	
Uyghurs	4.4%	5.9%	89.7%	

The new liberal political atmosphere has changed many things with regard to minorities and minority education. The policy of learning from the workers and peasants was gradually abandoned and school graduates were no longer sent to the countryside for re-education. Instead, we were encouraged to learn scientific knowledge at school. The old Communist ideals and heroes, such as Lei Feng, were no longer promoted and went out of fashion very quickly. The university entrance examination system was reinstated and we were strongly encouraged, or even coerced, by our teachers and parents to study hard in order to pass the exams so that we could secure a university place and, eventually, respectable employment in the state-owned sectors.

The new heroes were the founders of modern sciences such as Sir Isaac Newton and Chinese mathematician Hua Luogeng, and a few child prodigies who passed the university entrance exam at a very young age and were regarded as geniuses. The old Uyghur writing system, which was based on the Arabic script, was reinstated as the standard for the Uyghur language; the New Uyghur Alphabet, which was based on the Pinyin system and introduced just before the beginning of the Cultural Revolution, was gradually phased out.

Uyghur cultural and religious identity and practices were tolerated and started to return to centre stage at Uyghur schools and other public institutions in the region. While most school textbooks were still trans-lated from the standard Chinese texts used across China into Uyghur, the literature textbooks were rewritten and Uyghur literary works and intellectual traditions were given major prominence. The very existence of many of these works introduced in the Uyghur literature was un-known to most Uyghurs who had been born and grown up since the Communist takeover of China in 1949. It was the first time I learned about Uyghur literary and historical works, from the 7th century Turkic inscriptions from northern Mongolia and Central Asia to well known and popular contemporary works by Uyghur authors.

Following this trend, numerous historical Uyghur and Old Turkic writ-ings were edited, published and disseminated among the Uyghur intel-lectuals and within educational establishments, even though many of them contradicted the official version of Xinjiang and Uyghur history (Bovingdon and Tursun, 2004). Uyghur writers became very active and created numerous literary publications, and many state-aided Uyghur language publishing houses were set up. Some Uyghur intellectuals and historians openly started asking questions about the official version of history and about the social, political and economic inequalities be-tween Han and other ethnic minority groups that existed in Xinjiang (Almas, 1989; Shabdanuli, 1982; Otkur, 1985).

Uyghur and other minority ethnic political leaders were promoted to important and powerful positions and the role of the Uyghur language rose in importance in political, social and economic life. A whole new generation of Uyghur intellectuals who were very aware of their own cultural, literary and linguistic heritage and traditions started to emerge; they grew in confidence and took pride in their culture, language and history. Religion was given renewed emphasis and religious education started to emerge in unofficial circles.

The intellectual class had started looking beyond the borders of China in order to explore the Uyghurs' historical, cultural and linguistic links with their ethnic brethren further west in Central Asia and beyond (Chen and Pan, 2000). Foreign films and other entertainments proliferated in cinemas, music venues and on television screens. Imported products, such as TV sets made in Japan, fridges and winter clothing from the Soviet Union, were in very high demand and they all looked far superior in quality and style to their domestically produced counterparts in China. Owning foreign products became not only a practical necessity but also a cultural and social status symbol in society. Tourists from Europe and North America began to visit the region, and traders from Pakistan and Central Asia started importing products from their own countries and selling and buying goods in shops and markets across the towns and cities. People began to realise the importance of learning foreign languages and communicating with the outside world.

While these new developments were seen positively and welcomed by the majority of the Uyghur population, especially the intelligentsia, they inevitability intensified the friction with the Han ethnic group and were not welcomed by them. They had the potential to create and promote a Uyghur ethnic national identity, based not only on cultural and linguistic grounds, but also on a different political allegiance to the one that was promoted by the Chinese Communist Party.

It was in this wider context that I completed my secondary school studies. I became intensely interested in learning science subjects and worked hard to achieve good results in examinations. I learned Uyghur literature and language and started composing poetry and short prose pieces in Uyghur; I learned about Uyghur history and cultural heritage and thought about my own Uyghur ethnic identity and its relationship with the rest of China. I became conscious of the dynamic power relationships that existed among the various social, linguistic, cultural and ethnic groups in Xinjiang; I developed an interest in the world beyond the borders of China. I set myself a goal of working hard to achieve the best results possible, not only for myself, but also for the honour of my people. I became frustrated by the very limited learning material and resources available in the Uyghur language, particularly in science subjects, and was determined to improve my Mandarin capabilities as soon as I could get the opportunity.

University education and beyond

The national university entrance examination which was held once a year was a crucial event not only in the lives of students taking the exam, but also for their parents and families, as a pass guaranteed the student a job for life, an 'iron rice bowl' after graduation. While revising for the university entrance exam at secondary school, I learned how hard it was to pass the exam. We had to take several rounds of qualifying exams before reaching the final, and it had been rare for students from my home town to pass the final round in the previous few years. Corruption in the system was rife and many good students who did not have family connections with government or education officials, or could not afford to pay them big enough bribes, were disqualified in the locally-marked early rounds. I had neither the family connections nor the money to pay the bribes; I felt it was a miracle when I learned that I had survived the qualifying rounds to reach the final national examination. Then, just before the exam period started, both my parents had serious health problems and the family found itself in a very difficult position. In these circumstances, I could only hope to achieve an examination result that would enable me to go to a local technical college or a teacher training university.

When the exam results were announced, I found, to my great surprise, that I had achieved one of the highest marks in the whole province and was accepted by a top university in the capital city, Beijing. I suddenly felt I had become the centre of attention in the whole town; everybody was looking at me in a different way as I went past on my old bicycle. All the important leaders from my father's factory came to our house to congratulate my father on my exam success and they offered to pay my travel costs to Beijing because I had brought honour to the factory.

I set off on an epic journey of more than 4,000 miles from my home town to Beijing. The first leg of the journey was to Urumqi, the provincial capital with a train service to Beijing. I travelled with my older brother in his goods lorry. His main purpose was to deliver packed cotton to a textile mill there. It took five days to reach Urumqi. I took the train from there to Beijing, sitting on a hard seat for three days and nights before reaching my final destination.

As I had taken my university entrance exam in Uyghur and my Chinese language skills were not up to standard, I had to start with a language preparation class at the university. All my classmates belonged to ethnic minority groups in Xinjiang; there were many different nationalities and they spoke several different languages. This was the first time I had encountered a situation where I needed to communicate with others in a language other than my mother tongue; it was the beginning of a life journey which continues to this day.

I studied hard to improve my Chinese in the language preparatory class and started learning English in my spare time, listening to the classes broadcast by the local radio station in Beijing. I acquainted myself with some spoken Kazak and Mongolian languages and became interested in learning and comparing different languages. But a real shock came when I went outside the campus to do some shopping and go to the post office to post a letter. First, I tried to explain to the bus conductor where I wanted to go but it took a while before she could understand what I was trying to say; once I arrived at my destination, it became even worse. It was an embarrassing experience for me and my self-esteem went down quite considerably. I felt that there was a real gap for me to fill in terms of knowledge and language skills and I was determined to achieve that as quickly as I could.

One morning, when I went out for a run in the university sports ground, I met a European-looking person. I was curious and eager to talk to him, so I decided to try to use the English that I had just learned from the radio broadcasts. It was very difficult for us to understand each other, but it was a pleasant exchange for me and we made arrangements to meet again. We met regularly after that, despite the strict university rules about not talking to foreign students without permission. We exchanged greetings and managed to have a short dialogue to start with; our exchanges became longer and more friendly as time went by. I invited him to my class parties, which he seemed to enjoy very much. After a few months, the European student returned home, but we kept in regular touch by postcards and letters for a number of years. This contact further stimulated my interest in learning the language and learning about Europe and the English-speaking world in general.

When I finally started my degree programme in psychology after finishing the language preparatory programme, I found that I was the only student who was a non-Chinese mother tongue speaker in a class of 35. Everyone seemed to speak in a different dialect and it was difficult for us to understand each other, as the students came from many different provinces and regions of China. I started attending a four hour a week compulsory English language module as part of my degree programme; this was taught throughout all four years. The teacher had a limited command of English herself and she avoided speaking English in the class except when reading out the vocabulary or sentences from the textbook. Progress was slow and the teaching not very effective, but I decided to try hard by myself and went out every morning before classes started to memorise a paragraph in English from a textbook. Every Sunday morning, I went to the local English Corner to practise my spoken English there.

Our psychology class was one of the few in the country. Regarded by the Communist Party as a fake science and against Marxist principles, the subject had been banned for over a decade. We were taught mostly about advances made in psychology in the Western world and I began to read widely about Western intellectual trends and theories. It was all new and inspiring to me and I made good progress in understanding the theory and practice; my determination to travel to the West to study the subject became stronger than ever.

After graduating from university, I returned to the provincial capital city, Urumqi, to teach psychology at a university. There I met an English couple who were teaching English in the foreign languages department. Very quickly, we got to know each other well and met up regularly for social events or English Corners. After hearing of my enthusiasm and desire to study in a Western country and the difficulty for me in obtaining the necessary funding and permission from the authorities, the couple offered their help. They went back to England a few months later and sent me a course acceptance letter from a university in London, together with a supporting sponsorship letter. I used these to obtain my visa from the British Consulate.

Becoming a linguist at an English university

After obtaining the visa and other necessary permission from the authorities, I decided to travel by land through the Central Asian republics of the then Soviet Union and Russia and from there on to Europe in order to reach Britain. The decision to take the land route, rather than to fly from Beijing to London, was to reduce the travel costs. Although I did not know in advance what might be the cost of travelling by land all the way to Britain, and other possible complications, it turned out to be a very lucky decision. It was very soon after the failed August coup d'état by the Soviet Army to oust the reformist government led by Mikhail Gorbachev when I arrived in the Soviet Union. The coup leaders may have failed, but it seemed the whole political and economic system had collapsed.

I saw that every daily necessity was in short supply when I arrived in Almaty, the capital of Kazakhstan; the shop shelves were empty; there were long queues everywhere for bread and other essential food supplies; black markets were flourishing for all these things. I was astonished to see at first hand that the Soviet Union – a country which we had been told was one of the two advanced First World imperial powers along with the United States – was in such a desperate condition. The only thing that still appeared to be working relatively well under state control was the railway system, with its prices set by the state at the time.

I spent a few weeks in Almaty trying to sell fake Adidas sports clothes which I had brought with me from Urumqi. They were snapped up quickly by middlemen at premium prices on the black market. With the proceeds, I felt, for the first time in my life, that I was richer than the average person in that society. I bought a ticket for a luxury berth on a train from Almaty to Moscow – a journey of several thousand miles – for 70 Soviet roubles, which was the equivalent of £1.50 at the unofficial exchange rate. In Moscow, I saw similar scenes to those in Almaty. After waiting for three days, I finally managed to buy a ticket from Moscow to London which included both the train journey and the ferry across the North Sea, all for 400 Soviet roubles, which was about £6 at the black market exchange rate. The cheap prices were due to the state price controls on transport – which were lifted soon after I left the Soviet Union.

While travelling through the Central Asian republics, I encountered many different languages and cultures. I discovered that the Turkic languages spoken there were not difficult for me to understand. I was able to find my way quite easily using the transportation signs and was able to follow the announcements in the metro system. I found that basic spoken communication with the local people was possible using my knowledge of the Uyghur language. The only challenge for me was the Cyrillic writing system. So I started learning the Cyrillic script and Russian. By the time I left the Soviet Union after more than a month of travelling, I had managed to gain basic communicative skills in several of the languages.

After arriving in London, I resumed my studies. It was a long held dream come true and was one of the most exciting periods in my entire life. I studied psychology at first and then economics. I continued with learning the Central Asian Turkic languages and studying the region in general. When the Soviet Union was dissolved in late 1991, several independent states were established in the region and started to gain international prominence. I thought I was in a unique position, being fluent in Chinese as well as having a good knowledge of several Turkic languages of Central Asia when there was a shortage of such skills. I started looking out for opportunities. On one occasion, I was asked to translate an official letter from the British firm, Rolls Royce, to the government of Kazakhstan.

It was by chance that I saw a small notice in a corner of the notice board in the university library for a temporary curator's post at the British Library which required my language skills. I decided to apply for the post without having much expectation, but a few weeks later I was invited for an interview and was offered the job. At about the same time, my language skills helped me to get a job as a freelance producer at the BBC World Service producing radio programmes in Central Asian languages. I enjoyed both these jobs and learned a lot.

My fluency in Central Asian Turkic languages had improved greatly and I began to develop an interest in the cultures and cultural exchanges between Chinese and the Muslim world, influenced by my exposure to the extensive historical material housed in the British Library. I began keenly seeking further opportunities to utilise not only my language skills, but also my wider cultural, historical and sociological knowledge in order to fulfil my dreams even more.

Two years later, an opportunity arose for me to work in Durham University for six months. It gave me an opportunity to use my language skills in both Chinese and Turkic languages. I started to develop my knowledge in other languages, such as Arabic, Japanese and Turkish. I began to interact and collaborate with academic colleagues who were experts on the region as well as in the languages and cultures. A few years ago, one such academic colleague and friend, Anwei Feng, encouraged me to start researching language education policies and multilingual and multicultural societies in China. I am now developing my expertise in this area and enjoying my work with Anwei on a research project to investigate trilingualism and trilingual education for ethnic minorities in China. I currently work more widely with several languages of Asia and the Middle East. It has been exactly fourteen years since I arrived in Durham and I now regard Durham as my home. I have already spent longer in Britain than in my home province of Xinjiang and in a couple of years' time I will have spent longer in Durham than in my original home town.

It has been a long, complicated and difficult journey since I left Kashgar at the age of 16 to go to university in eastern China, and then to travel abroad to the UK to study. I miss Kashgar, its people, its environment and its culture, but the journey I have embarked on to chase my dreams has been very worthwhile and I never stop raising the level of my dreams every time I reach a destination. I continue to make new goals and new dreams for myself. I now begin to feel that this might be my mission in life and I enjoy pursuing my goals and dreams tirelessly.

Notes

1 A mass movement in China (1966-1976) through which Mao Zedong hoped to perpetuate the Communist revolution and recover his waning political control. His assault on the Chinese Communist Party (CCP) became known as the Great Proletarian Cultural Revolution. It is estimated that between 400,000 and half a million people died as a result of the Cultural Revolution. The policies pursued in China since the late 1970s rejected everything that the Cultural Revolution stood for but it still casts a long shadow over the country. It was officially described in 1981 as having caused 'the most severe setbacks and the heaviest losses suffered by the Party, the state and the people since the foundation of the People's Republic' (*Major Documents of the People's Republic of China, December 1978-November 1989*, p160, cited in Townson, 1999).

6

A doctoral student in Manchester: becoming an independent learner

Xiaowei Zhou

I am a female doctoral student specialising in intercultural communication. In my doctoral research, I explored the academic acculturation experiences in the UK of a number of postgraduate students from mainland China (Zhou, 2010). I conducted my study through narrative inquiry (Clandinin and Connelly, 2000). In face-to-face interviews, I invited the students to tell their academic experiences in the UK in story form, and looked for insights into their academic acculturation in these stories. While I was reading their stories, I noted much of interest that resonated in various ways with my own experiences as a student. Because of our shared transition from mainland China to the UK we had many experiences in common. However, my research has also given me the perspective that we are all culturally-complex individuals (Holliday, 1994; Singer, 1998) who go through varying transitions in different ways.

I begin this chapter by reflecting on my learning journey as a culturally-complex individual. The following story is about my experience of becoming an independent learner through cultural transitions. My story reveals how my understanding of culture transcends national boundaries. The cultural transitions I went through involved a complex series of transitions between national and non-national contexts. It is through these various cultural transitions that I have become increasingly independent as a student, research student, and researcher. So I consider these cultural transitions to be the significant turning points in my learning journey.

More specifically, I tell my story of learning through these cultural transitions as my awareness of academic independence evolves. I start with my secondary-school years, when I developed an initial interest in the English language and follow my learning journey through the transitions from my home town to Beijing, from undergraduate to postgraduate education, from mainland China to the UK, from teaching-focused education to research-focused education, and from an apprentice culture to a professional culture. Through these transitions, I learned to cope with academic and non-academic culture shock as a sojourner. I became aware of my responsibility for managing my studies actively and flexibly. I learned to identify my own areas of interest, design my study plans accordingly, and position myself among diverse academic views. I became more able to make choices about my own research creatively and with reflexivity. I realised that to become an independent researcher, I should not only acquire necessary academic expertise and skills but also pursue this dream with courage and self-assurance.

My initial interest in the English language

I grew up in a medium-sized city in southern mainland China. During those years, most inhabitants in the city were locally born and raised, like me. I learned to speak the local dialect and developed similar culinary preferences to those of many local people. I had not seen many people from places other than my home town, but I had some second-hand knowledge about what people living in other cities might be like. This knowledge came from media descriptions and the accounts of my family members and relatives regarding their own experiences outside our town. I was intrigued to learn about the different ways of thinking and behaving of people living elsewhere.

This interest grew during my secondary school years, when I started learning English systematically. From the start, I had a flair for this foreign language. While my peer students were struggling to memorise the vocabulary and grammar, I found it easy to remember these things through acting. At that time, I thought I was acting in the language, because I was a non-native speaker of English and thus I was playing the role of a native speaker of English by using their language. Although this distinction between acting and actually using the language looks artificial to me now, it was a powerful motivation for my English learning during those years.

I found much joy in such role-plays, especially when I began to watch English films as soon as VCD rentals became available in my home town. These films were transformative for me. They made me realise the beauty of the English language. I became aware of the different accents between my teachers' English and the native speakers' English as well as the accents among the native speakers. I noticed many interesting words and expressions which were used by the film characters but were not included in my textbooks. I subscribed to several English-learning magazines and bought VCDs of my favourite films, such as *Gone with the Wind*, *Waterloo Bridge*, *The Lion King*, and *Titanic*. In particular, for me, the year 1997 was the year of *Titanic*. Attracted by this film, I watched it more than 30 times and read the film script again and again. I could remember almost all the lines. Loving the film so much, I felt really good when I acted out the script. This self-initiated exercise improved my English skills remarkably. My vocabulary was expanded. My pronunciation was more polished. Above all, my overall sense of the English language sharpened.

During my secondary school education, I stood out with my excellent performances in the English classes and tests. When I completed my studies there, I applied for the most prestigious English institute in mainland China without any hesitation – the English Department of Peking University. My hard work during the secondary school years paid off. In the summer of 1998, I received an offer from my dream university.

The transition from my home town to Beijing

Thus, at the age of 17, I left my parents and travelled northward to Beijing for my university education. My first impression of cosmopolitan Beijing was 'I do not belong here'. Adaptation was a big issue for me during my initial months and perhaps years in Beijing. I noticed a variety of differences between myself and other individuals, who were either locally born or came from other parts of mainland China. The differences I noted included those regarding food preferences, accents, ways of speaking, and even worldviews. In particular, I felt that many Beijing locals spoke loudly and tended to speak to non-locals in a rude and arrogant manner. Feeling lost, I wondered whether I could feel at home in this city. I appeared unconfident when speaking to individuals with a local accent. Later, during my studies, I found that my initial experience in Beijing was akin to culture shock (see Oberg, 1960), even though I was in my home country of mainland China.

Nevertheless, after I arrived in Beijing, I appreciated communicating directly with people from different parts of the country. I enjoyed meeting individuals speaking different dialects and hearing them talk about their experiences in their home towns. In addition, for the first time in my life, I was amazed to see people from abroad walking in the street. I even had the chance to talk to some of these foreigners and practise English with them. The oral English classes in my department were taught by native speakers from the USA and the UK. In my interactions with these language tutors, I realised that I was no longer acting in English, a language which I thought belonged to the native speakers of English. Instead, I was actually using the language as a non-native speaker of English to communicate with other people. Years later, during my doctoral studies, I read in the literature about the separation between using English as a first language, second language, foreign language, and global language (Crystal, 2003). I found my previous experiences of acting in and using English resonated with this academic discussion by echoing the foreign language and global language perspectives.

During my undergraduate years, when I started using English as an instrument for communication, I began to feel obstacles in speaking the language. To me, speaking English no longer meant performing a well-rehearsed text, such as reciting dialogues or paragraphs from the textbooks and acting film scripts. Rather, it was a process of improvising sentences to express my own thoughts. Improvisation was not easy for me as a novice English speaker, although I had already been an English learner for six years.

During my studies at Peking University, I received expert training in the English language. I learned to pronounce words and read sentences in English in an approximately native way, based on an understanding of the different parts of the tongue and throat that Mandarin and English speakers use and their different habits for tones and rhythms. I practiced my spoken English skills with my native English tutors and peer students and undertook extensive writing exercises. As I progressed to the second year of study, I began to focus on the subject areas of English literature and linguistics.

From the very first day of studying in the university, I realised that the relationship between teaching staff and students was different from my secondary school. At middle school, students were closely monitored by the teachers. During school time, students were not supposed to engage in anything beyond their academic agenda unless the teachers gave them special permission. A concrete example is that students were required to stay on campus during school time, and there were guards at the school gate to enforce this regulation. However, I found that at university, the university gate was open all day, although there were guards for security purposes. There were no longer any head teachers. No-one would interfere with my decision to leave the campus at any time. No-one would check my daily homework and monitor my progress during term time. There were only course instructors and examiners whom I met in classes and examinations. In short, I became much freer.

Nevertheless, the sense of freedom meant that I had to monitor my own progress and regulate myself in planning my academic and non-academic life. When I was at secondary school, my study goals were simple: to get high marks so as to gain access to a good university. As a university student, my goals changed. I wanted to develop myself as a person and make real progress in my studies by enhancing my English skills. I hoped to become a competent professional in the English language and develop a career in an English-related area. Therefore, I gradually learned to study independently. I disciplined myself to spend a few hours each day on my course work. I borrowed reference books to aid my studies with or without guidance from the lecturers. I bought additional vocabulary books to learn more English words on top of those taught in class. I even studied during my school vacations, which I had rarely done in secondary school.

Development of my academic independence was accompanied by coming to terms with the foreignness I found in Beijing. I became used to the local accent and began to see local people's loudness as something normal rather than rude. I learned to interact with others inside and outside the campus in appropriate and confident ways. There were still some unpleasant experiences, but I never felt lost again. I began to accept Beijing as my home.

During the final year of my undergraduate studies, I attended a course titled 'Intercultural Communication'. I found the course very exciting and enlightening, because it reminded me of my personal adjustment to life in Beijing through my exploration of concepts such as culture shock, cultural stereotypes, and intercultural adaptation. I studied the other English-related courses with effort and interest, but I followed this course with passion! It was during this period that my academic interest in intercultural communication germinated.

In summary, during my transition from my home town to Beijing, I learned to cope with culture shock as a cross-city sojourner. I became aware of my responsibility to manage my studies actively and flexibly. In 2002, I obtained my Bachelor's Degree in English Language and Literature and decided to stay in my second home city and continue with my studies of English. I became a postgraduate student in the same academic department, specialising in English linguistics.

My transition from undergraduate to postgraduate education

During my three-year postgraduate studies at Peking University, I did not perceive much significant difference from my undergraduate studies until I attended the course 'Research Methodology'. This course was my first experience of learning to do research. It provided me with an opportunity to feel, through practice, the process of undertaking a complete research study, from choosing a research focus, to writing a literature review, and then to data collection, analysis, and report writing-up. I developed some initial knowledge of quantitative and qualitative research methods and learned to use data collection and analysis techniques such as interviews, observations, and SPSS.

As well as guiding me through the process of undertaking research, this course alerted me to a different kind of academic independence. During my previous university studies, the lecturers had always given me clear directions, for instance to deepen my understanding of the course contents and to develop my speaking, listening, reading, and writing skills in English. I realised that, as a research student, I was responsible for choosing a direction for myself. When the professor, the course tutor, asked me what research topic I would like to explore for the course assignment, my mind went blank. I was overloaded with ideas. I realised then that I was so used to having my direction specified by others that I could not find a specific topic to focus on. After I finally decided on a topic, I confronted and then coped with the issues of looking for related literature that suited my needs, designing my study for my purposes, and implementing the study with my skills and capacities. After completing this task (Zhou, 2003), which later received positive feedback from the professor, I achieved a great sense of fulfilment: this was really *my* study!

For my Master's dissertation, I conducted a more elaborate study (Zhou, 2005), in which I further developed my research skills. This study and my first piece of research for the course assignment both built on my interest in the phenomenon of intercultural communication. Fascinated by the power of interpretive inquiry, I gradually developed a preference during these two studies for exploring individuals' sense-making interpretively and qualitatively.

To sum up, during my transition from undergraduate to postgraduate studies, I learned to make plans for my academic studies by identifying my broad areas of interest and designing research studies that addressed my interests, preferences and practical considerations. I became aware that there were no longer directions set by the teaching staff. Instead, I needed to find directions for myself and then seek guidance and advice from the teaching staff, whom I used to call 'teachers' in secondary school.

My romantic trips in the UK

During my final year as an undergraduate student, I met my future husband in the university. When I continued with my Master's education in mainland China, he went to the UK for his Master's and then doctoral studies. During the years when we were living in two countries, I made regular visits to him in the UK during my university vacations.

These became my initial experiences of being abroad. My visits lasted from two to five weeks, and my experiences varied hugely between these visits. In general, my experiences as a romantic visitor to the UK resembled my transitional experiences between my home town and Beijing. However, I experienced culture shock in the UK in a different way, as the experience seemed to be split between my different visits over those years.

My first visit was a fantastic honeymoon period. I travelled with my husband to different cities as a tourist, feeling excited about seeing the historical sites and natural scenery, trying local foods, and communicating with the friendly British people. I compared my perceptions of mainland China and the UK. I was impressed with the advanced facilities in many aspects of UK society and the politeness shown by many people in the street, which seemed to me to be lacking in mainland China.

My experience during my second visit was drastically different. This time, my husband was busy with his studies, so I spent most of the time alone in his rented room. I felt lonely as I had no-one to talk to. When I went shopping, I was frustrated to realise that, as a postgraduate student majoring in the English language, I could hardly understand the English spoken by British people. The difficulties I had were not only with accents, but also with word usages which sounded foreign to me. I wondered: what did 'cashback' mean? Why did people say 'I know' when I greeted them with a comment on the nice weather? Why did the staff in fish-and-chip shops ask me if I wanted salt and vinegar on my chips when I was used to ketchup? What should I say when I was in a public lavatory and someone tried to open the door because they thought it was unoccupied? I had not learned such things from my English classes in China. I began to doubt my English skills and even my ability to manage my everyday life.

My third visit was somehow a turning point. This time, I had an academic task: my data collection work for my Master's dissertation. With my husband's help, I accessed some students from mainland China as my research participants. Apart from our research relationship, I established personal relationships with them. They invited me to their homes and gave me valuable advice about things to do, places to visit, and ways of dealing with accents in the local area. These experiences reduced my sense of loneliness significantly.

In my following visits to the UK, I learned more about the local cultural context and became more competent in managing my everyday life without feeling marked discomfort. I stopped comparing my experiences in mainland China and in the UK. Rather, I began to accept the differences between the two countries in a more neutral way, developing an appreciation for the good things and a tolerance for the less desirable aspects of both countries.

In summary, the ups and downs I went through during my visits to the UK provided me with an impressive experience of the complex yet exciting issues involved in intercultural communication and made me determined to become a researcher in this field. I wanted to learn more about this phenomenon and help people who live, study and work across cultural boundaries, and I was attracted by the UK as a country of history and cultural diversity. So after I graduated from Peking University, I applied to undertake doctoral research in intercultural communication in the UK. I was honoured to receive a scholarship from the University of Manchester and in late 2005, I came to Manchester to start my academic sojourn.

My transition from mainland China to the UK

Since coming to Manchester, I have had my first long-term experience of living in a different country as an academic sojourner. I had never visited Manchester during my romantic trips. However, having experience of living elsewhere in the UK, I did not feel as excited upon my arrival as I had during my early trips. I found that my knowledge of the UK could be usefully applied during my stay in Manchester.

Nevertheless, there were still a range of things which I found new and challenging, particularly in my academic life. During my first year of study, I was required to attend a set of research training courses and earn my access to independent doctoral research. I had problems understanding the lectures I attended, although I recognised that the lecturers all spoke English clearly. But I found it difficult to capture their key arguments and follow their logic. In addition, they tended to teach by providing handouts during each session and asking students to consolidate what they had learned by reading relevant materials after the session. Such a mode of teaching provided me with little opportunity to prepare for the lectures in advance.

Sometimes the in-class handouts included substantial interview data extracts. The lecturers asked the students to 'spend a few minutes' reading these extracts and then discuss them with each other. However, the extracts were often lengthy and full of local expressions which I was unfamiliar with. When my peers from English-speaking countries were ready to discuss the materials, I still found myself struggling to digest the meanings of what was written in the materials. The situation worsened when the lecturers taught with video clips which contained news reports and interview programmes produced locally.

During these research training courses, I was part of a student cohort made up of students from various countries, including Africa, India, mainland China, Taiwan, and Korea. In the classroom, my peers from the UK, Africa, and India often volunteered to ask questions and express their opinions. Their insightful and humorous interactions with the lecturers made the lectures very enjoyable, but I could not always understand what they said. I often struggled to keep pace with the lecturers as well as my peer students. I was uncomfortable about being unable to participate in their interesting discussions, as this made me feel undesirably different from students from the English-speaking countries.

I noticed that I was not alone in feeling this way. The other students from Asia tended not to speak in the classroom either. Some students from the volunteer group once asked me why my friends and I from Asia were so 'shy' in the classroom. I was surprised that my minimal oral participation was interpreted by them as shyness, as I really wished to speak. I found it hard to explain this apparent shyness: it was difficult to volunteer to speak due to the confusion and frustration I felt about my difficulty with the English I encountered in the classroom. I felt pressurised by my peers' fluency in academic English. This apparent language problem seemed to involve not only linguistic issues, but also culture-specific and subject-specific issues. For example, the native and non-native speakers had their idiosyncratic ways of speaking. They often used culture-specific examples to illustrate their ideas. Some lecturers organised their lectures flexibly, encouraging students to dominate the classroom discussion. I found that often I could understand each word they spoke, but had no idea what their sentences meant.

All these difficulties contributed to my academic culture shock as an international student. I was aware that my transition between different educational contexts was associated not only with specific countries but also with specific disciplines and study levels. I had not only travelled from mainland China to the UK, but also from literature and linguistic-based subjects to a social science subject, and from teaching-focused education to research-focused education.

By the end of the first academic year, my classroom participation had improved a little, though less than I'd hoped. I was more engaged with my independent reading and thinking. Nevertheless, the difficulties I came across gave me insight for my subsequent doctoral research. In addition, my accumulated understanding of the relevant conceptual and methodological areas gradually enabled me to exchange my thoughts more fluently with critical friends. I participated more actively in seminars held in my department. At the end of the first academic year, I wrote and presented a paper in collaboration with a British peer at an international conference (Smith and Zhou, 2006), and the paper received positive responses from the audience.

To sum up, during my initial academic transition from mainland China to the UK, I experienced difficulties in my studies. I felt dissatisfied with my classroom participation and uncomfortable about being considered by my peers to be shy. I chose to concentrate on my independent work, and gradually made some progress in my communication with English-speaking academic peers. With my sound initial training in research methodology at Peking University and my hard work during the first year in Manchester, I accomplished the course work with excellent marks and progressed to my doctoral research.

My transition from teaching-focused education to research-focused education

My institutional base in a School of Education added a new dimension to my interest in intercultural communication. For my doctoral re-

99

search, I focused on the academic aspect of the intercultural communication experiences of students from mainland China, including their acquisition of new rules and behaviour in their host academic surroundings in the UK. During my research, I had individual tutorials with two supervisors and these differed from the experience of attending lectures. Perhaps due to the individualised and face-to-face nature of the tutorials, I found my supervisors' English relatively easy to understand. I felt more relaxed and able to ask them questions and discuss my opinions with them.

I gradually noticed that my supervisors held different positions and perspectives over many issues, due to their academic specialisms and personal preferences. Although they did share similar views on conducting educational research within the qualitative paradigm, they sometimes disagreed with each other over certain concrete aspects of my study, such as how to approach Chinese culture, a key notion I discussed in my thesis, and how to conceptualise my research participants' mood status vis-à-vis academic acculturation. On a number of occasions, my research plans as agreed by one supervisor met with disagreement from the other.

The supervisors' differing views posed a big challenge to me as an early-stage research student. It taught me a lesson: the academic world is characterised and developed by varying voices. I became aware that as a research student, I should go beyond the acquisition of established knowledge, such as what culture shock means. I needed to find my own position among the various voices. For example, rather than seeking concensus regarding the definition of culture shock, I asked myself: what are the different understandings of this concept and which traditions shall I follow? The tutorials gave me good practice in thinking independently in this regard. I have benefited a great deal from this, particularly in relation to my exploration of the literature, where I found much debate around the key hooks in my study, including the notions of culture, intercultural communication, acculturation, Chinese culture and the practice of narrative inquiry.

During my doctoral studies, I have gradually developed the habit of being critical and reflective on my work through my in-depth immersion in the research methodology literature, discussions with my supervisors, and engagement in various kinds of academic activities. I learned to identify the particular positions underpinning each writer's arguments. I learned to make decisions for my research and ask myself why regarding each decision. Yes, I continue to read literature written in English ... and wait! Is this literature neutral or does it convey any kind of Western bias? Is there any discussion in my mother tongue which proposes alternative views regarding my conceptual foci and research methodology? Why am I reading these papers and not the others? Yes, I want to explore my participants' academic acculturation ... and wait! Why do I prefer the notion of acculturation to other related ones such as adaptation, adjustment and cultural learning and what are the differences between these notions? Yes, I would like to generate data with my participants through interviews ... and wait! Why do I prefer the form of face-to-face interviews to other data generation methods such as questionnaires and diary writing?

This wait-and-why habit ran through my whole research process. I came to understand that undertaking social science research, at least in my field, is not merely about heading out to the field, coming back with data, and examining the data with some taught techniques. Perhaps more importantly, it involves the researcher's critical thinking, creativity, willingness and effort to contribute to her or his field. It is important that each step taken by the researcher and the linkage between the steps is well informed, planned, and reflected on.

In my research, I was fortunate to have six kind and collaborative participants, who generated very rich and insightful data with me for a whole year. Their data allowed me to identify many interesting patterns with regard to their academic acculturation, such as their apparent academic isolation and the underlying reasons for this, their personal growth whilst in the UK, and their particular academic characteristics as family-funded only children born after the 1980s vis-à-vis prototypical descriptions of Chinese students.

Upon reflection, during the past six years, I have undertaken two related studies on the intercultural communication experiences of individual students from mainland China. These studies have many aspects in common, such as the case study approach, similar numbers of participants, and the general interview method. However, these two studies, which resulted in my Master's dissertation and doctoral thesis respectively, were clearly different in terms of depth, rigour, and contribution. Thus during my transition from a taught student to a research student in the UK, I learned to position myself among diverse academic views, rather than follow any established knowledge. I enhanced my ability to make decisions and choices for my own research with creativity and reflexivity. If my Master's education introduced me to what research is like, then my doctoral research experience has taught me about all the complexities involved in rigorous academic research.

My ongoing transition from an apprentice culture to a professional culture

At the end of my doctoral research, I attended my viva and had an unforgettable exercise there. One of the examiners made a major criticism of the research approach adopted in my study, ie narrative inquiry, and required me to return to my thesis and strengthen my discussion of this approach. I felt surprised, confused, and frustrated. Why did he feel uncomfortable with this approach? Did I use the wrong approach or misunderstand it? Why did my peers who used this approach receive no such criticisms from their examiners? Which part went wrong for my examiner and how should I address it? I spent some time recovering myself and then studied the examiner's comments calmly. After careful thinking and discussions with my supervisors, I realised that this criticism did not point to any flaws in my study, but was an invitation for me to explain my position more clearly to a reader who comes from a different field and is unfamiliar with the narrative inquiry tradition. I should stand my ground, but give more careful consideration to my readers' needs.

This exercise made me realise that to become an independent researcher, it is not sufficient just to learn how to undertake research. It is important to position oneself confidently in an academic world constituted by a wide variety of views. After all, the aim of undertaking research is more than producing a research report for its own sake. Researchers want to disseminate their work and contribute to the wider academic circle, which means that their work will be read, discussed, and critiqued by other scholars who may come from different fields. As I point out in my thesis, my study was built on interdisciplinary insights and I embrace the interdisciplinary characteristic of academic discussions of culture, intercultural communication, qualitative methodology, and narrative inquiry. However, as a doctoral research student, an apprentice academic, am I ready to confront challenges from interdisciplinary colleagues when I step out of my supervisor-nurtured comfort zone?

My viva experience alerted me to the issues involved in my transition from an apprentice researcher to an independent researcher. I look forward to becoming a professional academic in future. I have now realised that to become an independent researcher, I should not only acquire the necessary academic expertise and skills but should pursue this dream with courage and self-assurance.

Epilogue

Looking back, as an individual who grew up in mainland China and then travelled to the UK for doctoral education, I have had complex cultural and intercultural experiences which made me more than a Chinese student. I have been learning to become an independent learner through a variety of cultural transitions, including those from secondary-school education to university education, from mainland Chinese education to UK education, from studies at Master's level to doctoral level, from one disciplinary home to another, and from an apprentice culture to a professional culture. These cultural transitions, as well as the specific cultural contexts, shaped my thoughts at different stages and provided me with different insights with regard to where and how I plan to position myself in the academic world. The ups and downs, pains and gains I have experienced are a valuable pool of wealth that I can draw on now and in the future. I have learned to plan, manage, and monitor my studies with competence, independence and self-assurance. Looking forward, I am pursuing, with passion, my dream of becoming a professional social scientist. I am eager to start a career through which I can contribute to an understanding of the human world and from which I will achieve great joy and fulfilment.

7

A post-doctoral researcher in Hong Kong: 'I am not who I used to be'

Wenli Wu

In May 2009 I went back home to Wuhan and met friends I had not seen for ten years. Most of them told me their lives were almost unchanged, so they did not have much news to report. On the other hand, they were interested in what had happened to me, especially during my years in England. Sharing my overseas experience with old friends reminded me of the meaningful days I spent in the UK. It also gave me an opportunity for self-reflection to consider my future development.

Looking back, I realise that nobody lives in a vacuum. Everybody is influenced by their particular social, cultural, educational and political context. People have a propensity to behave in a certain way, but this can be reinforced by the environment. On the other hand, the environment is perceived in different ways by different individuals. As Williams and Burden (2000:192) point out, 'learners' perceptions and interpretations of their environments will affect their learning rather than the actual physical characteristics of those environments'. For Williams and Burden, what appear to be physical barriers to one group may be regarded as acceptable norms to other groups. In a sociocultural environment, many factors, such as the politics and the weather, are beyond the control of those who experience them. Yet some personal factors, such as attitude, are under one's own control. For example, if an individual is willing to change, with effort, he or she can become proactive, open-minded and tolerant – attributes which all contribute to a smooth cross-cultural adjustment.

I told my friends that I had changed significantly after so many years studying and living in England, although, the changes were not obvious from the outside. I am clear who I am and I have become more independent. I am more positive about life and believe that where there is a will, there is a way. Discovering my social identity and becoming more independent are two great achievements I derived from my life overseas. These are the aspects in which the seven years in England most changed me.

My motivation to study abroad

Studying in England was one of my biggest dreams since I was a teenage girl in China. At the age of 12, when I was a first year junior high school student, I started to learn English. My English teacher gave me lots of praise when I did well in class. I was motivated to learn English and to find out more about English culture.

When I was at high school my English teacher introduced us to a textbook called 'New Concept English' as supplementary reading material. In the second volume, one lesson was about a 'Famous Clock'. In it there was the following passage:

> When you visit London, one of the first things you will see is Big Ben, the famous clock which can be heard all over the world on the BBC. ....Big Ben takes its name from Sir Benjamin Hall who was responsible for the making of the clock when the new Houses of Parliament were being built. It is not only of immense size, but is extremely accurate as well.

I was fascinated by Big Ben when I read this passage. In the picture next to the text, the clock looks like a castle with a square face. Why is the clock extremely accurate? How can people all over the world hear it strike the hour? How immense does it look in real life? As a teenager, I had so many questions but it seemed nobody could answer them at that time. In those days it was very difficult for a mainland Chinese to go abroad, so nobody could describe Big Ben to me. The 'Famous Clock' became more mysterious when it was inaccessible. From that time on, just to have a look at this famous clock in person became a fervent dream for me.

Before I came to England, I was a qualified English teacher and had taught for four years in high school. I loved my students but sometimes I felt my knowledge and skills could not help me solve all the problems I faced at work. At this time the dream of going to England resurfaced. Rather than just having a look at the famous clock, my dream became more practical. My new aim was to have better competence in English.

In order to realise my dream, I took a risk and quit my job (which was regarded as an 'iron ricebowl' – a job for life – in China). In the late summer of 2001 I went to England to study for a Master's degree, having chosen Warwick University because the course of study there suited me well. I did not know what kind of life was awaiting me. I just wanted to chase my dream when I was still young. Therefore, I was highly motivated to make the most of life at Warwick because I had dreamed of this opportunity for such a long time.

My first year in England – encountering challenges

Before I went to England, my image of the country was very vague. There was no direct connection between my knowledge of England which I had learned from a textbook and what I actually experienced there. I just expected that I could study theories in the field of English language teaching and would be able to speak excellent English after completing my Master's degree. Also, I expected to make friends with many native speakers. So, following guidance in the university booklet, my parents provided enough money to see me through my first year in England.

Three days after arriving, I attended a pre-sessional English language course, and found it a good orientation for my stay at Warwick University, as I built up some confidence in language learning. Like most of the other students, I spent a long time learning English on the pre-sessional course, as English was to be my major. I was introduced to necessary English study skills and received much useful feedback from my tutors after doing various exercises.

At that time I experienced culture shock and some language problems, and was disorientated for a period of time. Everything was different from the environment I had been familiar with. For example, when I first got a bus timetable, I did not know how to make sense of it. I could speak English, but I found the way people expressed themselves was different from the way I did.

Ten weeks later, I started my Masters' course and found accommodation on campus. I was lucky because I had good flatmates. It was a single sex flat and all of us were from Asia. Throughout the year we got along well. Each day I could have at least half an hour's conversation with my flatmates in our shared kitchen. The topic could be anything that we were interested in. One of my flatmates from Malaysia had a near native competence in English so she was our language consultant that year. When we could not understand each other, we used body language, drawings and a dictionary for better communication.

In my first term, I had difficulties with the academic courses. I found the teaching methods unfamiliar. When I was growing up in China, the teacher was the most important person in the classroom, and students followed the teacher's guidance. In England I found that students and teachers are in a more equal relationship, and often the teacher was the facilitator of learning. I felt lost and unsure as to how I should behave. For example, unlike in the Chinese education system where teachers always have the right answers, in England I was pushed to find the answer by myself. My MA tutors always pretended that they did not know anything but they gave us plenty of opportunities to think on our own. When necessary, the tutors gave us a lot of support so I could work out my ideas with support from them, but I was very uneasy in those early days because I was afraid that I would make mistakes and people would laugh at me.

I came to appreciate the student-centred teaching style and the informal, friendly relationship with tutors. For example, my dissertation supervisor invited me and his other tutees to his house for a barbecue, where we sat down together and chatted like friends. It had been impossible to treat my teachers as friends when I was a student in China.

Thanks to help from my friends and teachers, my sense of feeling lost did not last too long. At the initial stage of my overseas study, I met some senior students in the same department, and they gave me invaluable advice on academic and daily life. For example, in England at Masters' level many courses do not prescribe a textbook, while in most Asian countries every subject has a textbook. Hence note-taking and referring to tutors' handouts are more important when attending lectures in English universities. For daily life, practical tips like where to go shopping for special regional food, and how to find items at the best prices was the kind of information I was keen to have. Those senior students helped me adopt a number of strategies in my social and academic life, such as asking for feedback from proofreaders, using the internet to access material in the target language, attending social gatherings to improve my language skills and cross-cultural awareness, and so on.

At that time I discovered, with amazement, the power of new technologies. For example, I was introduced to the online database offered by the library, so without physically going to the library I could study in my room. Another example was learning to use an instant online chatting system to exchange information with my friends and family all over the world free of charge. Here lay the roots of my interest in doing doctoral research later on. In the first term I had problems because I read slowly and so I always finished my assignments in a rush. I had no time to ask people to proofread my work though I really wanted someone to do it for me.

During this term my flatmates took me to pubs and parties. I had never tried any alcohol in China because my father always told me drinking and smoking were immoral for girls. I was surprised to find that my Malaysian and Korean flatmates were heavy drinkers, and yet I was sure they were nice people! I ordered a glass of orange juice during my first visit to a pub but my Malaysian flatmate asked me to try some Baileys Irish Cream from her glass. It was sweet and tasty, and I liked it immediately. From that time on I started to have a small amount of alcohol every time I attended a party.

Aside from my flatmates, I learned a lot from my course peers. In the second term I had a team mate who was working on a project with me. She was from Hong Kong and had an extensive English vocabulary, which I admired. As she could not speak Mandarin Chinese and I could not understand Cantonese, we had to communicate in English. Doing the project in a team encouraged me to learn ways to express my meaning without causing offence. I found it was important because without knowing that strategy I would never have been able to cooperate effectively with my classmates.

In this second term, benefiting from writing assignments and reading feedback from tutors, I started to realise the differences between writing in English and in Chinese. I found that the Chinese style of writing favours indirectness and implicitness, but English writing is more direct – actually I preferred the direct way.

I realised what the difference was after I received a lower grade than I had expected. I felt that writing English assignments was the most demanding part of my Master's course that year because I had to do a large amount in a short time.

In the Easter vacation I found a part-time job as a cleaner with the university hospitality service. I learned how to use modern cleaning equipment, such as vacuum cleaners and mops. Lacking work experience in previous years, I was too tired to sleep well for a week. Nevertheless, I started to enjoy my work from the second week onward because I found I made friends with my workmates and I could practise English with them. It was great fun to get to know people from different cultural backgrounds while I was working.

During the third term of my first year at Warwick, I was busy doing assignments, looking for jobs and writing my dissertation. I had more worries about my future and study during this period of time. By the end of that year, I could talk more fluently in English with my flatmates, but not as well as I had expected. Looking back, I feel I was very lucky to have had such nice flatmates in my first year in England because I really learned a great deal. I feel that my parents' money was well spent because I could never have had such an experience if I had stayed in China.

In general, I enjoyed my first year in England, though my Master's course was very demanding and I had problems at different stages. I was pleased with my heavy workload because this made me feel that I had not wasted my tuition fees. In my spare time, I enjoyed the social life and I went to parties if I could manage the time. I liked sports and often played badminton with other Chinese students. Over the year I gained much confidence and developed my independence, which I appreciated greatly. I assume it was because I was far away from home so had to make all my own decisions. Gradually I got used to the fact that I was in charge of my own life.

Now I realise that these changes did not come about overnight. Rather I gained this independence through contact with a different academic and social culture. If I had stayed in China I would not have changed. I feel that the chance to get to know different people from all over the world enriched my personality because I had to develop my cross-cultural competence. Sometimes I had to change in order to communicate with people from other cultures. The more I learned, the more confident I became.

My other days in England – tears and flowers

If I could use a metaphor to describe my first year in England, I would say I was like Alice in Wonderland – everything was so fantastic for me. Nevertheless I was not satisfied with the improvement in my spoken English, and I thought one year was too short for me to really get to know British culture, so I decided to stay longer in England. Again, I did not know what sort of life was waiting for me.

After trying several part-time jobs in England over several months, I found I needed to equip myself with more knowledge for the unforeseeable future. As I had benefited from new technologies when I was doing my Master's, I decided it would be a great topic to research. In 2003 when I started to do my MPhil/PhD, my first interest was in exploring the relationship between Information and Communications Technology (ICT) and English language learning. However, my proposal was too ambitious, covering too many aspects – each aspect could have been developed into an individual PhD in its own right. I was challenged by my upgrade panel and urged to rethink my research focus, research questions and research methodology. I was very upset and disoriented when the panel asked me to resubmit a proposal within six months. I felt I was in a cul-de-sac. What would I do if the panel thought I was not qualified to be a PhD candidate? How could I face my friends and family, who were waiting to see my title changed to 'Dr Wu'? I was haunted by all the 'what' and 'why' questions and I could not sleep for several days. I did not dare to tell my family the result of my upgrade application.

Fortunately I slept well after a long chat with a friend. I realised it was no use crying over spilt milk. My supervisors and peers helped me to re-shape my research questions after I had received the formal suggestions from my upgrade panel. I worked day and night without a break because I was afraid of failure. Three months later I passed my upgrade after I had submitted a fresh research proposal. Now I was grateful to my upgrade panel as they set me on the right track at the right time, even though redrafting my proposal had been a very painful process.

The remaining days in England were never smooth. I had difficulty with my research from time to time; I had financial problems in my second year; and I had an argument with my family during the writing-up stage. Compared with other challenges, the frustrations of research were easy to handle because they were partly under my control. The financial problems perplexed me for more than six months but they were solved dramatically in the end.

The conflict with my family tormented me until I received my PhD certificate, and I cannot say this has yet been totally resolved. After staying in England for over five years, my attitude towards life and my conception of the world changed without my parents realising it. It was frustrating to try to explain to my family why I was behaving in certain ways, within the constraints of a weekly half-hour telephone conversation. My pain came from the fact that I care deeply for my family and wanted to please them all the time. Our argument started at the end of my fourth year's study when I told them I did not know when I would be able to submit my thesis. They were furious because they thought I was not working hard enough when I was far away from them.

Nevertheless, the strategies I learned in my first few years helped me overcome all the obstacles before I finally reached my goal. Three years after my upgrade, I was awarded a Doctor of Philosophy in Education by the University Senate House. On my graduation day, my friends gave me a bunch of flowers to celebrate my success.

In October 2008, I flew to Hong Kong to join my fiancé, who had waited for me for years. Before leaving, I visited London again and took photos of Big Ben, the famous clock, from different angles. For so many years the picture of Big Ben had been deeply implanted in my mind. Good-bye, Big Ben! Good- bye, England! Now I need to chase my other dreams in China.

Reflections on my life in England

It has now been one and a half years since I left the UK, but the places where I stayed, the people I met, and the happiness and sadness I experienced are still vivid in my mind. In general, I feel fortunate that I made the decision to study in England in my twenties. I find that my outlook on life and the world changed after meeting people from over 100 countries. After reading the stories of other international students, I realised that mine is a microcosm of the experiences of thousands of mainland Chinese students studying in England at the beginning of the 21st century. We were fortunate because we benefited from the rapid economic progress and 'Open Door' policy in mainland China.

My experience was not unrepeatable. I was consistently influenced by my environment and my own character. There were internal and external factors which interacted in my life, and allowed me to have these experiences. By external factors I mean the situational or environmental factors whether opportunities or obstacles. In brief, the important external factors that influenced my life were academic related, such as tutors and the subjects I chose to study; and life related, such as my place of residence, the town I lived in and the friends I made.

External factors

Maslow's (1970) hierarchy of needs indicates that the basic needs of a human being, such as food, housing, and a safe and predictable environment, are the foundation of higher level needs (eg self-development). Accommodation is extremely important for international students because where they stay is their home during their studies (Lewins, 1990). My university was like a small town, so the shopping choices were limited. I liked to leave the campus and observe people's daily life but, because of financial concerns and a heavy study load, I just stayed on campus most of the time. The 'small town campus' was ideal for peaceful study, but not that wonderful if one wished to experience real life in Britain.

Since everybody in my flat was from Asia, I could live comfortably without speaking complicated English. I received emotional and practical support from my flatmates as we shared similar cultural backgrounds. For example, we always cooked together and exchanged cooking tips. Needless to say, we all loved rice and fresh vegetables, and we all showed our sympathy for those 'poor' people who only ate cooked food and bread.

In many cases, the Chinese stomach is very sensitive. If Chinese people do not have appropriate food for some time, they feel ill. However, I could easily accept any type of food that I thought was delicious. Because of financial concerns, though, I had to cook for myself almost every day. 'What shall I cook today?' was a tough question for me as I had little prior experience of cooking. I learned basic everyday cooking out of necessity to satisfy my hungry stomach.

I did not learn much about the British way of life in my first year because I was living in an 'Asian Town'. As a result, my spoken English did not improve as much as I had hoped. On the other hand, my academic performance was better than I expected, partly because I had close contacts with my academic tutors and received help whenever I needed it. I enjoyed the flexible British academic system. I found that I learned more from this than from the hierarchical relations with my teachers in China. My choice of subjects had an impact on my academic adjustment as well. When I was doing my Master's, I needed to write assignments in English so I had a deeper understanding of academic English writing and my written English improved more quickly than that of friends who did not need to write assignments.

Being in a new environment, my goal in the first year was to get my degree certificate and to learn academic knowledge which would enhance my competitiveness in the job market. I was keen to get to know people from another culture and to increase my cross-cultural competence, but I just did not have the time and energy to devote to these aims. That was why I decided to stay longer in the UK.

I was blessed in making many nice non-Chinese friends who provided generous help when I was in need. Among them, the two people who had the greatest impact on me were my landlady, Gill, and my life coach, Andrew. Gill is a kind English woman whom I had met in my first month in England. My life became different after I moved in with her in my second year. By staying with her, chatting with her, and attending social gatherings with other English friends, the British concepts of how to live life penetrated my mind without my being aware of it. Moving out of the comfortable Chinese community gave me an opportunity to see other perspectives in England.

Gill is a great listener, language instructor and grandma who cares for international students. I stayed with her when I was doing my PhD and she gave me enormous support. Many of my life philosophies came from her, such as 'Life is too short to regret' and 'Try your best, and think positively'. She introduced British culture to me. For example, at first, I felt very uneasy when strangers said 'Good morning' to me in the street. I did not know them, so why did they greet me? Would their greeting be followed up with some horrible trap? News reports which I read reminded me of all the possible negative explanations for the situations I encountered in the street. I mentioned my concerns to Gill and she told me it was the custom for English people to greet others. At the end of a conversation, many English people would say 'Have a nice day' to each other with a smile. Gradually, I found that to think positively and to have a happy mood at the beginning of the day was essential for me.

Meanwhile, Andrew introduced me to an understanding of my internal strength. He too is a good listener and has become a friend. When I complained that some tasks looked like 'mission impossible' and I might never finish them, Andrew always said 'if it is not difficult, then it is not worth doing'. He told me that everybody has a subconscious which could only recognise positive words. For example, if we say 'I do not want to fail the test tomorrow', our subconscious will interpret our wish as 'I want to fail the test tomorrow'. If you keep on thinking of 'fail', it is highly possible that you will fail. However, if we say 'I have tried my best, so I will pass the exam', our subconscious will accept our idea as 'I will pass the exam'. You may pass the exam in the end. It sounds a bit dodgy, right? Many of my Chinese friends said that the idea of the subconscious was just Western superstition! Nevertheless I have practised it and it really works for me! From my understanding, the essence of Andrew's preaching is: think positively!

Both Gill and Andrew are Christians. They took me to church and hoped that I would be as blessed as them by becoming a Christian. As a proactive way of learning culture I was pleased to know more about Jesus Christ but as a member of the generation who grew up under the red flag, I was taught that there was no God. Maybe because of this deep-rooted ideological teaching, I did not want to make a commitment to believing in God. My Christian friends respected my choice, and I read the Bible with them when I had the time.

In brief, it was mainly these external factors that had the greatest influence on my life in England. Coming to a new community presented me with many opportunities on the one hand, but frustrations on the other, because some opportunities were beyond my control. Having international classmates or flatmates could not ensure any instant improvement in my spoken English. Similarly, opportunities for feedback, which was helpful for language improvement and academic adjustment, may depend on what kind of teammates I was asked to work with on a project, with whom I was living, whom I met during everyday activities, as well as the enthusiasm of the tutor of a particular course.

Personal factors

Apart from environmental factors, attributes such as personality and motivation make the individual unique. Ryckman (2004) claims that personality can be defined as a dynamic, organised and uniquely held characteristic which makes an individual different from others in terms of cognition, motivation and behaviour in various situations. A succinct definition is given by Wagner (2005), who states that 'personality is made up of the characteristic patterns of thoughts, feelings, and behaviours that make a person unique'. In addition, she argues that 'personality arises from within the individual and remains fairly consistent throughout life' (Wagner, 2005).

By nature I was a very shy and introverted person, and I could not communicate effectively with others when I was in China. I dreamed of becoming more articulate and easygoing but I did not know where to start. In the first six months in England, talking with flatmates and other international students was a great challenge for me. Nevertheless I managed to change because I did not cling to my old ways of life. I developed a more open mind towards my new environment, and I was more willing to learn, to take risks and to make mistakes. So I was proactive and had more opportunities to learn new conventions which turned out to be helpful in my life. I was influenced by the environment surrounding me, and I consciously made changes.

One example is my working experience in England. For several years I worked part time at the International Office at Warwick University. Between 2004 and 2006, I worked every summer as a mentor on the pre-sessional English language course run by the Centre for English Language Teacher Education at the university. All my part time jobs had one common theme – they involved dealing with people.

My varied work experience enabled me to develop my interpersonal communicative competence, though I was not aware of this at first. In some circumstances I had to talk with hundreds of people in a day. It was often hard for me because by nature I was not an extrovert, but in order to do my job I had to learn to talk with people in a professional and polite way. I did not realise that I had learned those skills until I met other colleagues who told me that they had problems in communicating. Through practice I have found that the competence I developed in work and life has proved a boon in my overseas study. Trusting myself, believing in myself, and always having a positive attitude towards life allows me to see other aspects of life.

According to Kleinginna and Kleinginna (1981), the concept of motivation signifies the internal reason or condition that guides behaviour and gives direction. Many motivation theorists believe that a learning behaviour will not happen unless one is motivated. Two kinds of favourable motivations have often been discussed in learning: intrinsic and extrinsic motivation. Extrinsic motivation is 'when the only reason for performing an act is to gain something outside the activity itself, such as passing an exam, or obtaining financial rewards' (Williams and Burden, 2000:123). Conversely, intrinsic motivation is manifested 'when the experience of doing something generates interest and enjoyment, and the reason for performing the activity lies within the activity itself, then the motivation is likely to be intrinsic' (Williams and Burden, 2000:123). It is generally believed that a mixture of intrinsic and extrinsic motivation prompts many of our actions (Williams and Burden, 2000).

For me, to realise my dream and to become a better person were intrinsic motivations that pushed me to go further. Other drivers, such as never letting my family down, motivated me to study harder. The mixture of the two types of motivation has been the driving force behind my actions. Through all these years, I had always had a firm aim: to get my degree certificate, despite all the hurdles I faced. This aim was my motivation for study. It would be a disaster if I could not get my degree certificate in the end. That was why I was so depressed when I was asked to submit a new proposal for my PhD upgrade. At that time I felt that I was on the verge of failing.

As a Chinese person, my priorities were a result of cultural conditioning. I was like most of the other Asian students in England: our priority was to gain our degree certificate and then to master useful career skills. I considered this to be synonymous with personal development. This is consistent with Elsey's (1990:46) claim that 'overseas students have a pressing need, perhaps above all else, to return home with their inner satisfaction and the outward measure of successful academic achievement'. Here, the rationale in the ranking of learning priorities for me was obviously influenced by my cultural background, and is significantly different from that of many of my UK counterparts (Watt, 1980).

Epilogue

I have not yet had a chance to return to England, but the friends I made, the life-changing experiences I had, and the environment I enjoyed there are engraved in my mind. I know I am not the person I was. My overseas study experience has changed my life completely. If I had not gone abroad, I might have stayed in Wuhan and continued to work as a secondary school teacher. In that case, I might have fewer dreams because they were just dreams, and I could not keep having daydreams all the time. But now, since I have realised my biggest dreams, I still feel young at heart and keep having other dreams. Unlike before, I am independent and confident. In addition, I have learned how to turn my daydreams into reality.

8

A teacher of foreign language in Hong Kong: the centrality of language

Jesse Chiu Lai Yi

I was an ordinary girl before I studied in the UK. Studying there gave me a chance to see myself through other people's eyes. It also changed my views on learning. I think it was the method of teaching that spurred me to want to learn more. In addition, the people I met in different countries taught me that a clear goal is very important. I was fascinated by their stories and dreams. And then I created my own stories, which fascinated many people around me.

I still remember the days when I studied English in Liverpool. My English tutor wrote on the blackboard: 'The more you learn, the more you know, the more you know, the more you forget, the more you forget, the less you know, so, why study?' All the students in the room were stunned and speechless, because this saying was too true and so precisely expressed our feelings. We kept asking ourselves: 'Why study?' No-one could answer. Every time I studied new things, this saying would come to my mind.

I think I can answer this question now, after all these years of studying at different schools in different countries: we study to forget. Once you forget what you have learned then you will have space in your brain to learn more. I think this is the way our brain works. Even if we might forget what we have learned, the knowledge we have acquired always stays in our subconscious mind whether we want it or not. And one day those memories or knowledge will resurface. Our brain is like a computer, with primary memories and secondary memories. The primary memory will not be executed until you use it. Just like the computer, we have limited Random Access Memory (RAM). We cannot open all the applications we have stored at one time. We only open those we need or execute them automatically according to the situation. So I told myself not to be afraid of forgetting, and to keep on learning.

Childhood in China and Hong Kong

My mother and father were both born in mainland China to wealthy parents. They did not need to worry about their life before the war. But things changed very quickly once the war began. I think their school days and life values must have been greatly affected by the war and the Cultural Revolution. They started to work during the War of Liberation. In the old days, there was a saying, 'Do it, and you get 36, but you still get 36 even if you do not do it'. It meant that you got paid 36 yuan whether you worked hard or did nothing at your workplace. I think most workers thought this way at that time, including my parents. They were not so keen on education after the Cultural Revolution, especially as my father had been jailed because he was a painter during that period of time.

I was born in Ji'nan, the capital city of Shandong province in mainland China. I spent my childhood in Ji'nan and Shanghai before I migrated to Hong Kong. In the 1970s, children went to school from the age of 7. I was sent to some kind of nursery school both in Ji'nan and Shanghai. These places cannot compare to the nursery schools of today. I remember how boring it was. Children messed around, had a nap after lunch and then waited for their family to pick them up. No-one would teach you anything. Maybe they did, but I have no memories of learning anything, besides doing some drawing or colouring. Although I could see all kinds of musical instruments stored in the cabinet, no teacher could teach us how to play them. In the playground, I could see some ancient weapons like swords and spears for martial arts training. Again, no-one could teach us how to use them. I felt frustrated whenever I saw them. I was 4 or 5 years old at that time.

After a strong earthquake near Shandong province in 1976, two of my aunts from Shanghai came to persuade my mother to send me there, so that my mother could take care of my younger brother in case there were aftershocks. It was my first trip on an aeroplane. I then started my new life in Shanghai, a city that is very different from Ji'nan. The buildings are taller, there are more people, and the food tastes different. Everything seemed so new to me. I lived with my granduncle and his family. They taught me things like writing traditional Chinese characters and reading. Most people spoke the Shanghai dialect at that time, but I was only able to speak the Shandong dialect. My second language acquisition started with the Shanghai dialect at the age of 5. The Shanghai dialect is very different from that of Shandong. I did not notice this until my reunion with my mother and younger brother a year later. I really could not understand what my mother and younger brother were talking about when they came to pick me up at the train station. That was shocking, and made me realise that people speak different languages. Of course, like many children, I did not find this difficult and did not take too long to adapt to the new environment and to communicate in different languages.

Schooldays in Hong Kong

The third language I acquired was Cantonese. My father and my older brother had migrated to Hong Kong two years before the rest of us. At the age of 7, I had my first experience of being in a school where I had no idea what the teachers were talking about. It took me two months to understand and speak Cantonese with the help of my older brother, who taught me how to read Chinese characters in Cantonese. My parents were puzzled as to why I was able to read within such a short time. What they did not know was that my great-uncle and his family had already taught me many Chinese characters when I was in Shanghai. So learning Cantonese did not seem so difficult for me. I started to go to school from the end of May, which was almost the end of the school year. I spent less than two months in Grade 1 and was able to go on to Grade 2. I had no difficulty with any of the subjects except English. I was quite occupied with learning Cantonese, adapting to the different environment, and making new friends. English for me was like a language from another world. We did not use it in our daily life but needed to learn it every day.

In Hong Kong, we lived very close to my father's relatives in a suburban district. Most of our neighbours did farming, gardening or running a pig farm for their livelihood. They had inherited the businesses, houses and the land from their ancestors. This pattern was quite usual in the 1970s. They did not need much education to make a living, and some of them were illiterate. They sent their children to school because they wanted them to finish secondary school, get a stable job somewhere, and earn money. They never expected their children to go to university. Most of the children around were raised in this kind of environment. That is why I did not think learning was important when I was young.

Studying in Hong Kong was not a good experience for me. In primary school, I just did whatever I was told to do. I went to school because the Hong Kong government provided free education for nine years and all children of my age had by law to go to school. I did quite well in Grades 2 and 3. The teacher made all the students memorise part of the Chinese textbook every day, and if you did not do your work, you would be punished. Therefore, I always got almost 100 per cent in my Chinese exams. However, my grades got worse and worse from Grade 4 on-wards. I think it was because the Chinese teacher I respected had retired. My Chinese finally declined to the same standard as my English. I always got zero marks in dictation tests.

When I was in Grade 6, in a mathematics class, the teacher taught us how to use a calculator to do division and express the answer to four or five decimal places. I did not use a calculator at first; I worked out the answer by mental arithmetic. I got the answer quickly and accurately, but the teacher did not compliment me. Instead he angrily told me to do it again using the calculator. I was heartbroken. He should not have done that to me even though I had not followed his instructions. I was able to answer the question without a calculator, which I think was good. A child's heart is very fragile. I started to ask why I should study. What was wrong with using our brain? What if we do not have a calculator to hand? My primary school days ended with bad memories and bad grades.

My parents never expected much from us. They even allowed me to choose the secondary school I would attend, with one condition. It must be an Anglo-Chinese secondary school, where English was the medium of instruction. My father was a mechanical engineer working at the airport. He had studied Russian at secondary school in Shanghai but he did not speak English, which made it hard for him to get a job in Hong Kong. Sometimes he sighs when he talks about this, and wonders if it would have been different if he had been able to speak the language. I realised that English was very important.

Fortunately, I had a good English teacher in secondary school. I loved the way she taught. We learned English with playing cards. Although I did not know at the time what interactive learning was, I found her teaching really impressive. It was the first time I felt English was interesting, and I managed to get over 70 per cent in English in the first exam, which was only two months after I started secondary school. It was so incredible.

In our school all the subjects were taught in English, except Chinese Literature and Chinese History. It became easy for me. I did not like Chinese Literature, because I did not see the point of the lessons. We did not learn much about grammar but, instead, were asked to memorise passages in the textbook or other people's textual analysis or critique. Why should I care how people criticise someone else? Everyone should have their own opinion. Another thing I hated was that we had to write one or two whole pages to answer a very short question. People who wanted to get high marks just had to write down the content again and again. If you did not use the model answer, you would get low marks.

Chinese History was another subject I had no interest in. Four thousand years is just too long a period to study, and there were too many names and dates to remember. But my World History results were quite good. At that time, I realised that being spoon-fed information did not suit me, nor did the compulsory education system. Although my English was getting better and better, I still had no idea why we had to study. Sometimes I could hear a voice in my head telling me that I would be fine even if I did not study.

In Secondary 3, I started my revision the day before the exam. I revised all night and then went to take the exam. When I heard, 'Time's up. Pens down', whatever I had studied or memorised the previous night would disappear from my mind. Then I would go home to have a nap, and study another subject once I woke up. One week of overnight studies helped me become top of the class, a position I retained for the whole year, although I did not consciously try to do so.

Most schools in Hong Kong group the best students into one or two classes. In our school they were grouped into Class A and Class B. I was in Class C at that time. Sometimes, I think I am the kind of person who would not improve without competitors. If I had been in Class A or B, what would I have become? I doubt anyone could answer this question, even me. When I look back now, I find that the language used in learning really affects the way of learning for many people. And having a good teacher is extremely important. A good teacher knows how to develop your skills and guide you to your goal.

I chose to specialise in science subjects in Secondary 4 and 5 so that I would have less to memorise. At the end of Secondary 5, all the students had to sit the Hong Kong Certificate of Education Examination (HKCEE) in order to go on to Secondary 6 and 7. I got bored with revision, and was unable to concentrate. At home, I found a Japanese language course-book with cassette tapes. I flipped through the book and put on the tape just for a change of atmosphere. But I kept studying Japanese from that day on. I was able to read, write, understand, and speak Japanese within one month. My father was very surprised. He knew Japanese was not easy to learn, because he had studied it without success. The results of my HKCEE were not very good, so I decided to study Japanese, and had my father's full support.

After six months of studies in Hong Kong, I felt that studying there could not satisfy my desire to learn Japanese. Growing up in an ordinary family, I did not expect to go overseas to study. But finally, my parents, persuaded by my reasoned arguments, agreed to send me to Tokyo when I was 17. This experience taught me that if you want to do something, you need to tell the people around you, make them understand why you want it and get them to support you. There are many things you will not be able to do on your own.

Studying in Japan

I went to Tokyo a few months after the Tiananmen Square protests of 1989. I met an English man in a local gym. He was around 25 and had been studying in Beijing before the protests. Like many overseas students, he had fled Beijing and he did not want to go back to his own country for a while. So he chose Japan, which is near to China, so he could go back to China once the situation allowed him to. We talked in Japanese and English at first, but when I found out that he spoke fluent, flawless Mandarin, we started to talk in that language. To tell the truth, I had never studied Mandarin even though I was born in China, but had picked it up by conversing with classmates at school. The Englishman told me about his experiences in Beijing and Tokyo. I learned a lot from him, such as how to study a new language, how to spend money wisely while enjoying life overseas, how to use your spare time, and many other things.

I made many new friends in Tokyo. Most came from places in Asia, such as Taiwan, China, Hong Kong, South Korea and Australia. Two months after arriving, I got a part-time job; this was a common practice for overseas students. I was able to find a job in a famous company, Konica, through a stroke of luck. The father of one of my flatmates had a chain of shops selling electric appliances and photographic equipment, and Konica had photo developing centres in the shops. There is a Chinese saying, 'You rely on your family at home, but rely on friends when you are away'. I could not agree more. I worked twenty hours per week and was able to fund my daily living expenses in Tokyo. Since I had worked in a photo developing company in my spare time at secondary school, I was able to teach other overseas students how to do their jobs although our Japanese was not very good at the time.

I went to school from 9 am to 1 pm, and then to work from 2 pm. Having a job was a very important way for me to practise colloquial Japanese. We learned grammar at college and then I would practise with my co-workers. However, a year later, I realised I had not learned as much Japanese as I thought. Because I had learned most of the grammar in Hong Kong, what I had actually been learning in Tokyo was vocabulary. I remember that I looked up words in the dictionary for more than three hours every single night in the first few months. It was a nightmare and very tiring.

I decided to study French at night school along with an Australian girl, so that I could try to learn Japanese directly from Japanese people, in the same way that we learned our mother tongue. I found the French class very difficult, because we were in the beginners' level class when we should have been at preparatory level. My friend and I went to the classes with zero French, but our classmates had already learned the alphabet and some daily conversations. What was more, our teacher spoke Japanese and French in the class. Because Japanese draws a lot on European languages, sometimes we could not differentiate between the two languages. That three-month course was a whirlwind, but at least we learned some French. Some twenty years later, I still remember how to greet people and introduce myself in French. We did not continue our French because our level was so far behind the others. And I remembered that I had not come to Japan to study French. My parents were paying expensive school fees and I needed to work at learning Japanese.

During the last six months of my stay in Japan, some Korean classmates and I got to know some Japanese students from other departments in our college. They were studying English and planned to go overseas to obtain their first degree. We used to go out together for Karaoke, dinner, and other social events. I felt my Japanese improved a lot because of this. We chatted about many topics, such as current events in Korea, China, Hong Kong and Japan. We also talked about our dreams and the future. It took me one and a half years to reach the highest level in our college. The whole course normally takes two and a half years to finish. Most of my classmates stayed in Tokyo for further study in other colleges or universities. I initially wanted to stay on, but, in the end, I changed my mind and went back to Hong Kong to get a job. In those eighteen months, I mastered the Japanese language, made a lot of friends from different countries, and found out that having a dream or a clear target is the key to a successful future.

Work experiences

Thanks to my fluent Japanese, I was able to get a job at the age of 20, in a large Japanese organisation in Shenzhen, China, as a supervisor in the Production Department. The company provided three months' training in Japan to learn how to make an interface cable for computers. I learned how to use different machines to do different procedures, and how to do quality control. The most important aspect was learning the Japanese style of management.

This was almost twenty years ago. Factories in Hong Kong had started to move to Shenzhen. But Rome was not built in a day. Most parts of China had insufficient facilities or resources, not to mention problems of hygiene. Furthermore, there was no air conditioning in the factories and most of the machines produced heat. In summer it was hard to concentrate on work. In winter, there was no heating; cold air came in through the gaps in the windows and it was too cold to concentrate. Electricity and water were very limited. Sometimes we had to buy bottled water for washing when the water supply was cut off.

Luckily there were two restaurants in the district. One served Chinese cuisine and the other sold take-away meals. We ordered take-away meals for lunch and went to the restaurant for dinner. Sometimes we ate what we had brought from Hong Kong, as we needed to go back to the Hong Kong office to report to the General Manager every week. Staff from Hong Kong regularly brought canned foods, snacks and commodities to Shenzhen.

I left the job after a year and three months, because I found the working environment in Shenzhen unbearable. As my health was being affected, I decided to go back to Hong Kong to get another job.

I joined another well known Japanese company as a translator soon after my return to Hong Kong. Although I sometimes had to travel to factories in China to do interpreting for engineers, most days I worked in Hong Kong, doing paperwork. My translating skills improved a lot when I was with this company, through discussions with other translators. There were over 30 translators in the Hong Kong office. The company even had a translation department. The translators worked together and shared their experiences. With the knowledge I had gained in the previous company, I was soon in demand. Some department heads would come to my boss to ask to borrow me even though they had their own translators. A year later, I felt I knew more than the people who were holding the meeting or giving the speech. I realised that I had the ability to go further, so when one of my school friends called me and asked if I wanted to change my job, I agreed.

My next position was that of shipping coordinator in a new company, despite having no experience in shipping. However I was able to learn everything within a week from the other staff. The company employed me, an inexperienced young girl, because I spoke fluent Japanese, could do translation and understood Japanese management systems. I worked as assistant to the Japanese sales manager. As a result, I was headhunted by this sales manager when he started a new company a year later.

In the new company I worked as sales coordinator in liaison with National Panasonic, Malaysia. My job became more and more complicated because I had to control the materials, production schedule, quality, costs and delivery schedule. I was sent to Japan for one month's training. I learned how to make TV tuners and other products. I was trained in stock control, and total quality control systems. I made business trips to Malaysia every month to discuss the production schedule. I used my Japanese and Mandarin, but had no opportunity to use English at work for four years. So I started to go to the British Council to study Business English at night.

In 1997, I became bored with my job. I was offered the opportunity of working as an interpreter on a Japanese film being shot in Hong Kong. At first, I doubted whether I could do this, but their interpreter had lost his memory in an accident during the filming and they needed a replacement urgently. My older brother was working on the film and he persuaded me to help them. I took five days annual leave and the pay was quite good. A few months later, I had the opportunity to work for the Japan TV Broadcasting Company on a documentary about the handover of Hong Kong.

I decided to leave my job and work as a freelance translator. I did three movies and worked as a coordinator in Japan for about a year and a half. I earned three times more than before, but it was exhausting. Sometimes I only got three or four hours' sleep a night. I always worked under pressure and had no time to spend with my family. Eventually, I decided to find a job that allowed me to have a balanced life again. It was easy for me to get a job in production control, thanks to my previous work experience. I enjoyed it even though it was quite boring, because of the regular hours.

My peaceful life ended suddenly with a phone call. It was from a headhunting agency, asking me if I was interested in a new job. The head hunter told me about the reputation of the company, how good the pay would be and what benefits they offered. I refused at first. But the agent insisted that I go for an interview and finally I agreed. I accepted the offer because there was so much I could learn; it was a major company listed on the Hong Kong stock exchange, with many subsidiary companies. I was to work in the OEM (original equipment manufacturing) and ODM (original design manufacturing) business.

My manager spent two weeks teaching me about my daily duties, and then went on honeymoon for three weeks. By the time she returned, I was able to do the job independently. I worked on a project with department heads and had meetings with the customers. I was carrying out a manager's duties, although my title was Sales and Marketing Officer. Since my senior managers did not speak Japanese, I was the only one who could handle this project. People from other departments respected my work; the project was the most important in the whole organisation.

I intended to stay with this company for the long term. The only reason to leave would be to go overseas for further studies. I went back to college to do business studies at night; all the officers in our company had a degree. I was the exception, because they needed someone who could speak fluent Japanese and was able to manage a large-scale project. One day when I was chatting with my senior manager, I told her that I was so busy that I had worked until 10 o'clock the night before and totally forgotten to go to evening school. I was very upset when she replied. 'That's your own business'.

After two years it was time for my promotion review. Everyone was surprised that I was not promoted, including my former senior manager (the person who had given me this job but later left to take care of her son). I realised I had no future in this company and I decided to study abroad again. So I went to the UK at the age of 30. I started with a one-year English course, and then took another three years to obtain my Bachelor's degree.

Studying in the UK

Not long after I started my studies in the UK, an e-mail was forwarded to me by one of my cousins, which read, 'Imagine life as a game in which you are juggling some five balls in the air. You name them work, family, health, friends, and spirit, and you're keeping all of these in the air. You will soon understand that work is a rubber ball. If you drop it, it will bounce back. But the other four balls – family, health, friends, and spirit – are made of glass. If you drop one of these, they will be irrevocably scuffed, marked, nicked, damaged or even shattered. They will never be the same. You must understand that and strive for balance in your life' (Dyson, 1996). I totally agreed with this and gained confidence in my decision to resume my studies. I had spent ten years building my career, but finally found that it was not what I wanted. Study is about learning not only from schools but also from the people we meet, and about how people communicate and adapt to the changing world.

The thing I liked most in the UK was that tutors always guided students to do what they wanted. They never tried to limit your thoughts, but would try to help you when you were stuck. I remember one of my tutors in multimedia technologies course always reminding us that 'There is no reason why you cannot do this or that. Try whatever you want'. Another tutor from Marketing said, 'There is no right or wrong. But you need to prove your point to convince other people.' I loved the way students were allowed to be creative and interactive.

What changed me the most was one of the compulsory modules called Unique Learning. In the first week, we were asked to take five minutes to write down our goal, and then used SWOT analysis to find out our Strengths, Weaknesses, Opportunities and Threats in the second week. We had a lecture presenting the Reflections on Learning Inventory (RoLI) which helped us to recognise our learning style in the following week. And then in the fourth week, we were asked to write down a clear personal action plan with SMART criteria (Specific, Measurable, Achievable, Realistic, Time bound) to specify the goals, describe how to achieve them and provide a time frame for those goals. In the end we were asked to produce a Portfolio of Academic and Personal Action Planning about all we had done in the past few weeks. We had to rewrite the five minute goal statement in more detail, with a reflective 1500 word essay about the whole process. I had never written down my goal in the past. My entire plan was in my mind. But this module allowed me to understand that if you wanted to achieve your goal, you should write it down and analyse all its possibilities. I felt I had been reborn. I loved the studies, and I always tried my best to get an A grade. I felt upset when I got B grades.

I made a lot of friends who came from different countries and spoke different languages. The International Department in our university arranged regular gatherings for overseas students, so we had many opportunities to meet people from other countries, and to learn about their culture. I made many friends from South Korea, Japan and China. Strangely, I did not feel there was a generation gap between us. There were many mature students like me on the campus, which made me feel comfortable. Young students were quite happy to chat with me. Some of my friends told me a few years later when we met again that they saw me as their role model.

Studying Korean in South Korea

Studying in South Korea was one of my dreams. I planned to study in Seoul after finishing my Japanese studies in Japan. Unfortunately, the situation in South Korea was considered dangerous due to student activism, so I decided to go to Seoul and learn Korean after graduating in the UK. Having had experiences of overseas study in Tokyo, Liverpool and Cambridge, I thought Seoul would be a good place to study. I could see the desire to learn foreign languages in most of the students I met. Sometimes I felt they were too ambitious. It was as though if you did not keep on learning, you would be left behind.

My first experience of studying in Korea was at the Korean Language Institution (KLI) of Yonsei University for three months in 2005. I had wanted to study the language ever since I first met my Korean classmates in Tokyo. All the Korean students seemed to be very clever and always got good marks in exams. And then one day I finally understood why they were so successful – the grammar of Korean and Japanese is very similar, as is the pronunciation. It is like the similarity between Italian with Spanish.

I landed in Seoul with the little knowledge of Korean I had learned from my Korean friends in the UK. The first month was not easy for me even though I spoke fluent Japanese. Sometimes I tried to speak Japanese or English with the local people, but most of them did not understand me. What I liked most about the Korean people was that they would always try to find someone to help, or they would write Chinese characters to communicate.

Students in South Korea mainly stayed in a boarding house near their university. I found my boarding house through KLI. The house owner did not speak Japanese or English. Luckily, my floor-mate was an American Korean who was able to speak both languages fluently. She helped me to talk to the owner. There were thirteen girls in the same house, from three nearby universities. We usually had casual chats over meals. Most of the Korean students had three languages: Korean, English, and another that they had chosen in secondary school, such as Japanese, French, German or Chinese. This made me very envious. I remembered my old secondary school days – I always wanted to learn more languages rather than subjects I considered useless. I told my friend I would have got good grades if I had only studied languages for the HKCEE.

After three months, I went back to Hong Kong with many plans. But a plan is a plan. I got a job after two weeks, doing almost the same kind of work I had done before I went to the UK. I wanted to work in a European or American company, but my Japanese and my work experience prevented this. However, this time I was working alone, running the Hong Kong office for a Japanese company with factories in China. Although the job description was almost the same, I had the opportunity to work as an accountant. This at least was new for me. I was able to finish work on time almost every day, so I decided to study for a Master's degree.

Master's course in Hong Kong

I chose Japanese language and teaching for my Master's course, with a view to teaching Japanese after retirement. From Monday to Friday, I went to university after work and finished the course within nine months. Again, I made a lot of friends from different age groups on this course. There were native Japanese speakers, experienced Japanese tutors, fresh graduate students, and students from Taiwan and Beijing.

I have had many language acquisition experiences in my life, but when I became a teacher, I suddenly realised that teaching was not as easy as I had thought. There are students with different abilities and learning styles in every class. How to manage the classroom activities and atmosphere, and motivate students is difficult for teachers. However, I think the most important thing is not simply to teach the students a new language, but to teach them how to learn a new language. Students in Hong Kong are used to being spoon-fed, copying notes from the blackboard but never really using their brain to think about or digest what they are supposed to be learning. That is why people find it so difficult to learn a new language. I hope that one day I can write about my language learning experience or design a method for learning a new language in a more effective and efficient way.

I left my job and returned to KLI for further study. I had a clear goal in mind. I wanted to observe how tutors taught and how students actually learned in class. My plan was to study for six months. Unfortunately, there was a change of plan after three months. A friend of mine invited me to work for his company on some motion capture shooting projects in Tokyo. I was really interested as I had studied Multimedia Technologies in my BA, but never had a chance to use it in my work.

I went back to Hong Kong after the project was ended. I tried to get a job in the multimedia industry, but instead got an offer from a Japanese company to work as a project manager again. A year later, I felt that business was not for me. I wanted to do something meaningful. I had a flashback memory of a TV commercial I had seen in the UK. I saw many children with sad faces and heard the voice-over saying, 'Wanna help? Teach!' So I became a Japanese teacher, teaching in a Japanese language school. My time in the UK had not only changed my view on education but also given me my direction for the future. It seems every little thing has had an effect on what I would become, but I believe everything happens for a reason.

Learn from the past

I think specialising in one field is very important. My language skills earned me respect in my early twenties, and allowed me to work in different areas. They represent my future career. What would I be if I had not studied abroad in Japan? I cannot say, because it seems that my achievements started from studying Japanese. And studying in the UK gave me the chance to explore different ways of teaching and to understand myself more deeply.

I think learning is like practising yoga. Many postures are very easy to do, such as lying down on the floor and breathing. We were born with the ability to do this without thinking. But there are many postures you might not be able to do initially but, with constant practice, suddenly one day you find you can. If you gave up, you would never be able to do them. We should apply this theory to our lives. We can change ourselves through learning. The more you learn, the more you know or are able to do.

Studying in different countries and schools allowed me to meet different people and hear their stories and dreams. Therefore, my learning journeys will never stop and I will keep persuading people around me to study in different countries when they have a chance to do so. My learning journeys have changed so many people, who have been inspired to plan their own learning journeys and this has made me really glad.

9
Epilogue – realising the dream
Jon Nixon

Reading through these compelling accounts, I was reminded of the Chinese proverb: 'the wind got up in the night and took our plans away'. All the contributions to this volume bear testimony to the power of the night winds and to the fact that learning begins only when we awake to the realisation that the plans have indeed been blown away. Feng Su and the contributors to this volume have provided an invaluable service in making available such rich accounts of what learning means at the beginning of the 21st Century. It is only after the winds that, as Said (1997:34) puts it in his treatise on 'beginnings', 'there must be the desire, the will, and the true freedom to reverse oneself, to accept thereby the risks of rupture and discontinuity'. In this brief reflection on the significance of this collection, I want to set those ruptures and perspectives in some kind of provisional context, to understand what they tell us about learning, and what they envisage regarding our uncertain futures. My own reading of these fascinating chapters has, for me, been a wonderful learning journey.

The long march
In his preface to this volume, Feng Su alluded to the ways in which the 'Chinese learning journeys' documented in the previous chapters intersect with and have been shaped by the grand narratives of China's history over the last fifty years. This was a period of unprecedented social engineering during much of which the state has assumed

totalitarian control of every aspect of individual life. Dikotter (2010) has estimated that at least 45 million people died unnecessarily between 1958 and 1962 alone as a result of the Great Famine which was itself a consequence of Mao Zedong's Great Leap Forward. The Cultural Revolution that followed from May 1966 to October 1976 involved political purges across China, mass killings in rural China in particular, and what Walder (2009) refers to as 'the politics of institutional collapse' in the major conurbation (see also Esherick, Pickowitcz and Walder, 2006). The end of what Gray (2010:63) has called 'one of history's greatest experiments in terror' is usually dated as 1979, when China began its continuing process of opening up.

The authors of the preceding chapters are the survivors and offspring of that experiment. They are in the main, however, of a later generation that experienced Deng Xiaoping's 'Beijing Spring' and the subsequent liberalising reforms. That process of 'opening up' came to an abrupt halt with the state suppression of the Tiananmen Square protests that took place between 14 April and 4 June 1989 in response to the death of the reformist Hu Yaobang and the public demand to mark and mourn his death. As McGregor (2010) has shown, the Tiananmen Square massacre was followed by 'a purge of Stalinist proportions, albeit without a comparable body count at the end' (p36) and by a continuing policy of rigorous and largely covert state control through the apparatus of the ruling Communist Party.

In his influential analysis of the last two decades of Chinese history, Huang (2008) has identified a recent reversal of the revitalisation of the rural economy attempted during the 'opening up' of the 1980's. That reversal, he claims, has led to an urban bias in economic development which has in turn occasioned a widening of the inequality gap between rural and urban populations (see also Whyte, 2010). This has been accompanied by a closing down of public debate and a reassertion of the unquestionable and unaccountable authority of the single-party state. What Huang terms 'capitalism with Chinese characteristics' is defined by economic and political growth of epochal dimensions and by an apparatus of state control that cuts deep into the social and cultural lives of all China's citizens. It is the sheer scale of China as a land mass of 9.6 million square kilometres and a population estimated at

1.34 billion that renders the economic and political growth so globally significant and the apparatus of state control so difficult to relinquish.

The correlation between economic growth and growth in inequality is one of the defining features of the new post-1979 China. Using the 'Gini coefficient' (the measure used to compare international inequality in which 0 indicates absolute equality and 1 absolute inequality), Andreas (2008) shows how, between 1978 and 2006, China shifted on the scale from 0.22 ('among the lowest rates in the world') to 0.496 ('surpassing the United States and approaching the rates of the world's most unequal countries') (p136). In less than three decades China has moved from being one of the least unequal countries in the world to one of the most unequal. Moreover, while inequality between rural and urban localities has increased substantially, it is within localities – and particularly in urban localities – that the most severe polarisation of income has occurred.

These internal shifts and reversals have been accompanied by a re-positioning of China internationally. Hung (2009) has highlighted the deepening dependence of China and East Asia generally on the consumer markets of the global North as the source of their economic growth: 'Chinese and East Asian governments have employed their foreign reserves to purchase US debt not only in search of presumably stable and safe returns, but also as part of a deliberate effort to finance America's escalating current-account deficit, and hence secure a continuous increase in US demand for their own exports' (p17). This economic shift, argues Yang (2011a and 2011b), has had a serious and arguably deleterious impact on traditional cultural values as these are transmitted through China's higher education system. The position of China within the global order – and its orientation within that order – has shifted radically during the lifetimes of all those whose 'learning journeys' form the content of the preceding chapters.

The great diaspora

Those journeys are only part of the latest phase of a long history of migration that has created the great Chinese diaspora. That diaspora had its origin in the 19th century when colonialist expansion was at its height. Pushed by poverty and famine at home and pulled by emergent labour markets abroad, huge numbers of Chinese emigrated in search of an improved livelihood. From the mid-19th century onward, emigration was directed primarily to Western countries. Many of those who entered Western countries were themselves overseas Chinese from Taiwan or Hong Kong. When, in 1984, Britain agreed to transfer the sovereignty of Hong Kong to China, another wave of migration took place. The Tiananmen Square protests of 1989 further accelerated the migration. In recent years, China has built increasingly strong ties with Africa, occasioning a strong Chinese presence in a number of African nations, while the Chinese presence in the far east of Russia now forms a substantial proportion of the overall population of that region.

The contributors to this book are, then, part of a great and historic movement of Chinese people around the world. Their presence – like that of other migrant peoples – has contributed hugely to the local economies, cultures and societies of the countries to which they have moved or through which they have passed. The experience of some form of migrant labour is for many millions of people today the lived reality of globalisation: cosmopolitanism not as consumer choice or even value orientation, but as an unavoidable process of what Beck (2006:19) terms 'really existing cosmopolitanisation' (original emphasis). That process can be a deadening experience born of economic necessity; but it can also, as the previous accounts illustrate, be an experience that involves intense and transformative learning. For the contributors to this book it falls, in the main, into that latter category.

Those contributors now find themselves located in, or having moved through, a UK/US axis the economic standing of which has altered radically since 2007. As Hind (2010:4) points out: 'the peoples of Britain and the United States are now on the hook for more than thirteen trillion dollars ($13, 000,000,000,000). Money borrowed to rescue the banks has joined vast sums spent on weapons procurement and the steady enrichment of contractors against a background of escalating tax avoidance and evasion by the very rich.' On both sides of the Atlantic, strong and authoritative voices are warning against the dangers of premature fiscal tightening. (See, for example, McKibbin, 2010; Soros, 2010.) At the same time, as McGregor (2010:30) points out, 'there are now more billionaires in China than in any country other than the US'. The centre of economic gravity has shifted and with it the tidal flow of the global labour market. The previous accounts are, therefore, not only written in interesting times, but written by those who are interestingly placed – precisely because they are 'displaced' – in relation to these times.

Movement around the world is more transient (in respect of settlement), differentiated (in respect of individual trajectories), and accelerated (in respect of pace) than ever before. Friedman (2005:11) argues that we are now living in a third phase of globalisation in which the world is 'flat' in its interconnectivities: 'globalisation 3.0 [phase three] makes it possible for so many more people to plug in and play, and you are going to see every colour of the human rainbow take part'. The internationalisation of higher education may be just one among many indicators of this trend, but it remains a highly significant one, with over 2.8 million tertiary students studying outside their country of origin in 2007 – an increase, as Gu (2011:135) points out, of 4.6 per cent on the previous year and of 60 per cent on the figures for 1999. The movement of students is, moreover, matched by the transitional mobility of academic staff and what Yang and Welch (2010) refer to as 'the Chinese knowledge diaspora'. Friedman's 'flat' world is a world of incalculable mobility.

In terms of student mobility, however, the movement has tended to be in one direction: from East to West (with an almost eleven-fold increase in the first decade of the 21st Century in the number of Chinese students studying abroad). The result, as Cheung (2011) argues, has been that in higher education 'internationalisation' has all too often meant 'Westernisation' and has had the effect, therefore, of reproducing uniformity and conformity rather than reinforcing the impulse towards a transformative cosmopolitanism. Cheung goes on to argue, however, that this trend may be abating as the Universities of the East gain in research capability and thereby rise in the world rankings and as Western students begin to view them as a more desirable option. The steep hike in student fees within the UK makes the prospect of UK students studying abroad in some of the great economic and cultural capitals of the East much less inconceivable than it would have been a decade ago.

The grand narratives of exodus no longer hold true. It is, increasingly, the little stories of myriads of movements to and from locality, region, country, and continent that shape our shared experience of belonging – and at the same time that shared sense of not belonging – in a global world. Most of those stories remain untold. But those that are told impart important truths about the contemporary human condition. They speak not just to the experience of the migrant, hugely important though that is, but to a general sense of ambivalent belongingness: a sense of the shared experience of not belonging. We have, as yet, little idea of what kind of life-world will emerge from this shared experience of un-belonging. The previous accounts do, however, provide us with some important insights. They remind us that, if globalisation renders the world flat, it also constitutes a depth dimension whereby identity itself becomes 'cosmopolitanised' by its inevitable border-crossings.

Cosmopolitan learning

Cosmopolitanism, as I have argued elsewhere, is one of the great 'imaginaries' currently shaping higher education across the world (Nixon, 2011:51-65). The author of every chapter of this book has presented her or his learning journey as a cross-border journey: learning inextricably entwined with the identity of the learner as that identity develops through the experience of learning across boundaries. For the contributors to this volume, learning is clearly a process of realisation, not just of the self but of the self in relation to the world; a process whereby, as Nussbaum (2010:84) puts it, we aspire 'to a nuanced inter-disciplinary type of global citizenship and understanding'. Learning is cosmopolitan learning. As such, it requires a different ethic towards intercultural relations: one that, as Rizvi (2008:115) puts it, 'denies that our cultures are fixed and essentially distinct, and insists that the relation between self and others can only be understood dialectically and hopefully in ways that are cooperative'. Whatever dreams the authors of this book are chasing are realised in and through that changing relation.

Writing about the experience of Chinese students in the context of Australian higher education, Ryan and Viete (2011:157) evoke the notion of an 'intercultural third space between the one owned by a new culture and the one we feel we belong to (but see with new eyes)'. Crucially, they argue, this intercultural third space is where 'we construct our new voices and identities'. (See Gu, 2011 and Su, 2010, for studies of the Chinese student experience within the UK system.) The 'we' refers specifically to the international students of whom Ryan and Viete are writing, but in an increasingly globalised world of complex intercultural border-crossing the 'we' becomes all inclusive. The authors of this book are not engaged in a different kind of learning. Their learning journeys may have been steeper, more extensive, riskier, but it was not different from those of any other learners. The only difference lies in the authority with which they can – by virtue of that steeper, more extensive and riskier journey – teach us all about learning.

The extraordinariness of the journeys related in the previous chapters brings us back to the ordinariness of all human learning: to what is essential to the process of learning and what is non-negotiable regarding the conditions necessary for learning, and to what is intrinsic to the ends and purposes of learning. It is important to note, therefore, that many of the Western stereotypes of the Chinese learner are misplaced. As Li (2009:49) shows, the Chinese learner is, by tradition, predisposed towards a notion of learning as necessarily involving purpose (in respect of the learner's contribution to society), affect (in respect of her or his commitment), achievement (in respect of the application of knowledge), and agency (in respect of motivation). The desire to learn is, for the overseas Chinese learner, never a response to perceived deficit, but always a response to the potential capabilities of the learner. Those embarking on their various learning journeys bring to those journeys resources of hope and resilience – and extraordinary intellectual courage. They come not in deficit, but with largesse of potential, of promise, and of purpose.

What Western universities have to understand is that they too are learners in the great interchange that is occurring between the East and the West. That will be extremely difficult for Western universities which continue to fashion the idea of the university according to their own ideal. The 'academic drift' in the US, UK and increasingly across Europe is towards a model of the research-led university that is highly selective in its intake, largely independent of public funding, and fiercely competitive (Brown, 2011; Lazerson, 2010; Ritzen, 2010). This model of the university is hugely dependent upon the income derived from overseas students, but is wholly incapable of thinking beyond its own self-referential and one-dimensional notion of excellence (see Nixon, 2007). This inevitably limits the possibility of partnership through a shared understanding of the ends and purposes of higher education. The West, as Cheung (2011) has argued, is still unwilling or unable to learn.

That does not mean, however, that we cannot learn together and across boundaries. It simply means that we have to look elsewhere for our sources of learning. That is precisely why the previous chapters are so important: they point a way forward to new modes of inter-cultural understanding. In bringing together these narratives, Feng Su invites the readers of the book to become fellow travellers. He invites us to gain from these unique learning journeys an understanding of what is common to all learning. The questions this reader at least wants to address in encountering these narratives are: *What do they tell us about learning itself? About what it means to be a learner in the first quarter of the 21st Century? What do we learn about the experience of learning?*

We learn, first, that *learning is transformative*. Taking any of the previous narratives and starting from any point within those narratives, the depth dimension of learning is clearly in evidence. Learning transforms the individual's sense of self and sense of purpose. It transforms who we are and who we might become. The acquisition of skills, knowledge, and understanding is in itself *transformative*. All the learning journeys recounted in the previous pages testify to the fact that learning not only changes the learner, but changes the learner for the better through the broadening and fusion of horizons. Learning is never merely instrumental: a technical means to a pre-figured end. The ends and purposes of learning are only ever fully realised through the process of learning itself. As Deng Xiaoping is famously reported to have said, you cross the river by feeling for the stones at the bottom of the ford with your feet.

The capability approach as developed by Nussbaum (2000) and Sen (1999) and then applied to higher education by, for example, Nixon (2011:68-83) and Walker (2008) has a direct bearing on this notion of transformative learning. Capabilities – defined as the freedom to exercise our capacities – impact on our expectations; these expectations, in turn, create a need for the further development of our capabilities; and that growth constitutes human flourishing. We see this process of flourishing at work in the narratives that comprise this volume: the experience of learning that moves life beyond its given origins, notwithstanding the determining factors that constitute those origins, towards new beginnings, new horizons, and new peripheries that reinforce the power of human agency. Of course, the deep and multiple inequalities of life as lived in late modern capitalist society play inexorably against this benign view of human flourishing. But, somehow, it is the little stories of moving on and moving through that sometimes, against all the odds, earn a place in the alternative and as yet emergent narrative. Feng Su has begun to gather the resources of hope for that continuing journey.

Second, we learn that *learning is indeterminate*, by which I mean that its most vital outcomes can never be pre-specified. Of course, this claim runs counter to the audit culture that now dominates higher education with its endless demand for target-setting, outcomes-specifications, and clearly defined objectives: uncertainty, indeterminacy and irreducible complexity are simply unthinkable from the orthodox epistemological perspective which requires us to know what we will have learned prior to our having learned it. Yet, it is precisely the capacity for living and working together in uncertainty, indeterminacy and irreducible complexity that we require if we are to face the enormous challenges and opportunities of tomorrow. 'We need', as Patel (2009, 193-194) puts it, 'to see, value and steward the world in more democratic ways, realise that property and government can be much more plastic than we'd ever thought possible'. The previous accounts all testify to the importance of ensuring that there is a 'third space' for learning within which we can meet that need – and, in so doing, acquire the capabilities necessary to benefit from and contribute to human flourishing.

The moments of transition – of possibility, of opening up, and of interconnectivity – that structure and inform the previous narratives invariably take the reader by surprise, just as they took the authors by surprise when they lived through the events they are recounting. Chance meetings, sudden shifts of perspective, unforeseen opportunities: these are not peripheral to the stories, but constitute their very stuff and substance. In reminding us of the sheer indeterminacy and contingency of learning, the authors of this volume call the reader back to what Gadamer (2004, 298) calls 'the first condition of hermeneutics': namely, that 'understanding begins ... when something addresses us'. We cannot know in advance who or what will address us or, indeed, in what terms we will be addressed. The best we can do is to be ready and to be receptive. The previous pages provide ample evidence of how the authors on their various learning journeys were open to the indeterminacy of learning and responsive to the changing circumstances and unforeseen eventualities that constituted those journeys.

Unfinished journeys

Third, we learn that *learning is unfinished*. It is unfinished in the trajectory of a single lifetime, but is also unfinished in its impact on other contemporaneous lifetimes and on future lifetimes. Learning extends its influence across both space and time. Higher education as a system necessarily organises the limitless potential of learning into, for example, disciplines and fields of study, curricula and syllabi, points of entry and exit. It necessarily compartmentalises learning. The point of that compartmentalisation is to facilitate the thing itself: learning in all its transformative, indeterminate and unfinished potential. All too often, however, the system of higher education atomises the experience of learning. In its attempt to organise learning into manageable blocks of space and time, learning itself becomes distorted. Somehow, the contributors to this volume managed, in their different ways and often against the odds, to maintain the fluidity and permeability of learning conceived as lifelong and toppling into the future.

How did they manage this? How did they gather the necessary resources of adaptability and resilience? Part of the answer to these questions lies in what Appiah (2005) terms 'rooted cosmopolitanism', by which he means an outlook that is cosmopolitan in its recognition of different positions and perspectives while rooted in the particularities of local loyalty and community. A cosmopolitan outlook does not necessitate or even encourage an uprooting of affiliation and association from the partial to the universal, but does necessarily involve shifts of perspective. The contributors to this volume all have this capacity to gather the past into the future; to carry forward, and in so doing, enhance their legacy. Their origins (value affiliations, sense of belonging and of membership, etc) become more not less important to them as they define for themselves their new beginnings (expectations, prospects and promises, commitments, etc). Every reader of this book, regardless of their location or their origin, will have experienced at some time or other that sense of personal history as a forward movement into a fuller, more encompassing understanding of the past.

Relationship irradiates all the stories that are told in the previous pages. In some cases the strength of the authors' given, familial relationships is more strongly felt as they grow into the chosen relationships that characterise their new world. What we learn from these stories is that relationship matters, that individuality is incomplete without relationship, and that learning is always inter-connective and inter-personal. Good friends, reliable teachers, loyal colleagues and sometimes loving companions and partners are of supreme importance in the lives and stories of people who are on the move and on the edge. Their receptivity to and respect of relationship is one of the necessary resources of hope that sustains them on their unfinished journeys and that gives to their stories a sense of history in the making.

Towards the end of *The Memory Chalet* – an account of a learning journey written in the final months of its author's life – Judt (2010:207-208) wrote:

> We are entering, I suspect, upon a time of troubles. It is not just the terrorists, the bankers, and the climate that are going to wreak havoc with our sense of security and stability. Globalisation itself – the 'flat' earth of so many irenic fantasies – will be a source of fear and uncertainty to billions of people who will turn to their leaders for protection. 'Identities' will grow mean and tight, as the indigent and the uprooted beat upon the ever-rising walls of gated communities from Delhi to Dallas ... In this brave new century we shall miss the tolerant, the marginals: the edge people.

This volume gives me hope that, if the late, great Tony Judt is right about our entering 'upon a time of troubles', he may be wrong in assuming that there will be no 'edge people' to see us through. I think that in the stories here there is evidence of the continuity of 'the tolerant, the marginals', and that this evidence points a way forward to new forms of cosmopolitan learning. The challenge facing the university of the 21st Century is to provide the institutional and sector-wide conditions necessary for such learning to flourish.

References

Adamson, B (2004) *China's English: a history of English in Chinese education.* Hong Kong: Hong Kong University Press

Alexandra, L G (1993) *New Concept English.* England: Longman Group UK

Almas, T (1989) *Uyghurs.* Urumqi: Xinjiang Youth Press. (In Uyghur)

Andreas, J (2008) Changing colours in China, *New Left Review*, 54 (November/ December), p123-142

Appiah, K A (2005) *The Ethics of Identity.* Princeton and Oxford: Princeton University Press

BBC (2007) BBC web downloads set to launch. BBC, 27th Dec. http://news.bbc.co.uk/ 2/hi/technology/6245062.stm [Accessed 15/06/2010]

Beck, U (2006) *The Cosmopolitan Vision* (trans. C. Cronin) Cambridge: Polity Press

Bialystok, E (2001) *Bilingualism in development: language, literacy and cognition.* Cambridge: Cambridge University Press

Bolton, K and Kachru, B (eds) (2006) *World Englishes: critical concepts in linguistics.* London: Routledge

Bond, M (1991) *Beyond the Chinese face, insights from psychology.* Oxford: Oxford University Press

Bovingdon, G and Tursun, N (2004) Contested histories. In S. F. Starr (ed) *Xinjiang: China's Muslim borderland.* Armonk, N.Y. and London: M.E. Sharpe

Brown, R (ed) (2011) *Higher Education and the Market.* New York and London: Routledge

Cenoz, J (2009) *Towards multilingual education: Basque education research from an international perspective.* Clevedon: Multilingual Matters

Chan, C and Rao, N (2009) *Revisiting the Chinese Learner: Changing Contexts, Changing Education.* Hong Kong: Comparative Education Research Center, University of Hong Kong, and Springer

Chan, S (1992) Families with Asian roots. In E. W. Lynch and M.J. Hanson (eds) *Developing cross-cultural competence: a guide for working with young children and their families.* Baltimore, London, Toronto, Sydney: Paul H. Brooks Publishing

Chen, Y X (1999) Lost in revolution and reform: the socioeconomic pains of China's red guards generation, 1966-1996. *Journal of Contemporary China*, 8 (21), p219-239

Chen, Y and Pan, Z (2000) *Cultural insights into Pan-Turkism*. Urumqi: Xinjiang Peoples' Press (published in Chinese)

Cheung, A (2011) How Hong Kong universities balance the global and the regional: the challenge of internationalization, in B. Adamson, J. Nixon and F. Su (eds) *The Re-orientation of Higher Education: compliance and defiance*, Comparative Education Research Centre (CERC), The University of Hong Kong/Springer (forthcoming)

China Scholarship Council (CSC), Annual Report, 2009

Chinese Academy of Social Sciences, Ethnology Research Institute and China Minorities Comission (1994) *Survery of language use among China's ethnic minorities*. Beijing: China Tibetology Press (published in Chinese)

Chomsky, N (1968) *Language and Mind*. New York: Harcourt Brace and World

Clandinin, D J and Connelly, F M (2000) *Narrative Inquiry: experience and story in qualitative research*. San Francisco: Jossey-Bass

Confucius (1893) *The Analects of Confucius*. Oxford: Clarendon Press

Crystal, D (2003) *English as a global language* (2nd ed). Cambridge: Cambridge University Press

Cummins, J (2000) *Language, power and pedagogy: bilingual children in the crossfire*. Clevedon: Multilingual Matters Ltd

Cummins, J (1996) *Negotiating identities: education for empowerment in a diverse society*. Ontario, CA: California Association of Bilingual Education

Dikotter, F (2010) *Mao's Great Famine: the history of China's most devastating catastrophe, 1958-62*. London: Bloomsbury

Dyson, B (1996) The lesson of five balls. Address given at the Georgia Tech 172nd Commencement Day. Georgia Institute of Technology, Atlanta, Georgia, USA (6th September)

Eade, D (1997) *Capacity-Building: an approach to people-centred development*. Oxford: Oxfam GB

Edwards, J (1985) *Language, society and identity*. Oxford: Blackwell

Elsey, B (1990) Teaching and learning. In M. Kinnell (ed) *The learning experiences of overseas students*. Buckingham: SRHE and Open University Press, p46-62

Esherick, J W, Pickowicz, P G and Walder, A G (eds) (2006) *The Chinese Cultural Revolution as History*. Stanford: Stanford University Press

Fisher, C (2000) Partial Sentence Structure as an Early Constraint on Language Acquisition. In Landau, B, Sabini, J, Jonides, J, and Newport. E (ed) *Perception, cognition, and language*. Cambridge: MIT Press

Friedman, T L (2005) *The World is Flat*. London: Penguin Books

Fu, K (1986) *Zhongguo Waiyu Jiaoyushi* (A history of foreign language education in China). Shanghai: Shanghai Foreign Languages Education Press [In Chinese]

Furnham, A (1988) The adjustment of sojourners. In Y. Y. Kim and W. B. Gudykunst (Eds) *Cross-cultural adaptation: current approaches*. California: Sage Publications

Gadamer, H-G (2004) *Truth and Method*. (trans. J. Weinsheimer and D.G. Marshall) London and New York: Continuum (Second, Revised Edition)

García, O (2009) *Bilingual education in the 21st Century: a global perspective*. Wiley-Blackwell, Chichester

Gramsci, A and Buttigieg, J A (1991) *Prison notebooks*. New York and Oxford: Columbia University Press

Gray, J (2010) When no birds sing. *New Statesman* (20 September), p61-63

Greenhalgh, S (2008) *Just One Child – Science and Policy in Deng's China*. LA: University of California Press

Gu, Q (2011) Managing change and transition: Chinese students' experiences in British higher education, in J. Ryan (ed) *China's Higher Education Reform and Internationalisation*. London and New York: Routledge

Hayhoe, R and Liu, J (2010) China's Universities, Cross-Border Education and the Dialogue among Civilizations, in D. Chapman, W. Cummings and G. Postiglione (eds) *Crossing Borders in East Asian Higher Education*. Hong Kong: Comparative Education Research, University of Hong Kong and Springer, p77-102

Hayhoe, R (2004) *Full Circle: A Life with Hong Kong and China*. Hong Kong: Comparative Education Research Centre, University of Hong Kong

Hind, D (2010) *The Return of the Public*. London and New York: Verso

Ho, D Y F (1976) On the concept of face. *American Journal of Sociology*, 81(4), p867-84

Hoffman, M (1990) Beyond Conflict: Culture, Self, and Intercultural Learning Among Iranians in the United States. *International Journal of Intercultural Relations* 14, p275-299

Holliday, A (1994) *Appropriate methodology and social context*. Cambridge: the Press Syndicate of the University of Cambridge

Huang, Y (2008) *Capitalism with Chinese Characteristics: entrepreneurship and the State*. Cambridge: Cambridge University Press

Hung, H (2009) America's head servant: the PRC's dilemma in the global crisis, *New Left Review*, 60 (November/December), p5-25

Judt, T (2010) *The Memory Chalet*. London: William Heinemann

Kleinginna, P and Kleinginna, Jr. A (1981) A categorized list of motivation definitions, with suggestions for a consensual definition. *Motivation and Emotion*, 5, p345-379

Lazerson, M (2010) *Higher Education and the American Dream: success and its discontents*. Budapest-New York: Central European University Press

Lenneberg, H (1967) *The biological foundations of language*. New York: Wiley

Lewins, H (1990) Living Needs. In M. Kinnell (ed) *The learning experiences of overseas students*. Buckingham: SRHE and Open University Press, p82-106

Li, J (2009) Learning to self-protect: Chinese beliefs about learning, in C.K.K. Chan and N. Rao (eds) *Revisiting the Chinese Learner: changing contexts, changing education*, Comparative Education Research Centre (CERC), The University of Hong Kong/ Springer

Lin, A M Y and Man, E Y F (2009) *Bilingual education: Southeast Asia perspectives.* Hong Kong University Press

Mann, J (2007) *The China Fantasy: why capitalism will not bring democracy to China.* London: Penguin

Maslow, A H (1970) *Motivation and personality.* New York: Harper and Row

McGregor, R (2010) *The Party: the secret world of China's Communist rulers.* London: Allen Lane

McKibbin, R (2010) Nothing to do with the economy, *London Review of Books,* 32, 22 (18 November), p12-13

Nixon, J (2011) *Higher Education and the Public Good.* London and New York: Continuum

Nixon, J (2007) Excellence and the good society, in A. Skelton (ed) *International Perspectives on Teaching Excellence in Higher Education.* London and New York: Routledge

Norton, B (1997) Language, identity, and the ownership of English. *Tesol Quarterly,* 31, p409-429

Nussbaum, M C (2010) *Not for Profit: why democracy needs the humanities.* Princeton and Oxford: Princeton University Press

Nussbaum, M C (2000) *Women and Human Development: the capabilities approach.* Cambridge: Cambridge University Press

Oberg, K (1960) Cultural shock: adjustment to new cultural environments. *Practical Anthropology* 7, p177-182

O'Riagain, P (1997) *Language policy and social reproduction: Ireland 1893-1993.* Oxford: Oxford University Press

Otkur, A (1985) *Footprint.* Urumqi: Xinjiang People's Press (In Uyghur)

Pan, S (2011) Education Abroad, Human Capital Development, and National Competitiveness: China's Brain Gain Strategies. *Frontiers of Education in China,* 6 (1)

Patel, R (2009) *The Value of Nothing: how to reshape market society and redefine democracy.* London: Portobello Books

Pavlenko, A and Blackledge, A (2004) *Negotiation of identities in multilingual contexts.* Clevedon: Multilingual Matters

Ryan, J and Slethaug, G (2010) *International Education and the Chinese Learner.* Hong Kong: Hong Kong University Press

Ritzen, J (2010) *A Chance for European Universities, Or: Avoiding the Looming University Crisis in Europe.* Amsterdam: Amsterdam University Press

Rizvi, F (2008) Education and its cosmopolitan possibilities, in B.Lingard, J. Nixon and S. Ranson (eds) *Transforming Learning in Schools and Communities: the remaking of education for a cosmopolitan society.* London and New York: Continuum

Ross, H (1992) Foreign Language Education as a Barometer of Modernisation. In R. Hayhoe (ed) *Education and Modernisation: the Chinese experience,* Oxford: Pergamon Press, p239-54

Ryan, J and Viete, R (2011) Chinese international students in Australia: creating new knowledge and identities, in J. Ryan (ed) *China's Higher Education Reform and Internationalisation*. London and New York: Routledge

Ryckman, R (2004) *Theories of personality*. Belmont, CA: Thomson/Wadsworth.

Said, E W (1997) *Beginnings: Intentions and Methods*. London: Granta Books. (1st published in the USA by Basic Books, 1975)

Sen, A (1999) *Development as Freedom*. Oxford: Oxford University Press

Shabdanuli, Q (1982) Crime. Urumqi: Xinjiang Peoples' Press (published in Kazakh)

Shenzhen government online (2010) *Overview*. http://english.sz.gov.cn/gi/ [Accessed 15/07/2010]

Siegel, B (2007) Stressful Times for Chinese Students. *Time,* 12th June. http://www.time.com/time/world/article/0,8599,1631854,00.html [Accessed 10/07/2010]

Singer, M R (1998) *Perception and identity in intercultural communication*. Yarmouth: Intercultural Press

Siu, P C P (1952) The sojourner. *American Journal of Sociology*, 58(1), p34-44

Smith, P V and Zhou, X (2006) The dissonance between insider and outsider perspectives of the 'Chinese problem': implications for one of the UK's largest undergraduate programmes. Paper presented at the 2nd International Chinese Learner Conference, 15p-16July, 2006, Portsmouth

Soros, G (2010) The real danger to the economy, *New York Review*, 57, 17 (11-24 November), p16

Su, F (2010) Transformations through learning: the experience of mainland Chinese undergraduate students in an English university. PhD Thesis, University of Liverpool, UK. Thesis is available [on-line] in British Library Electronic Theses Online System (ETHOS) at http://ethos.bl.uk

Su, F, Nixon, J and Adamson, B (2010) Seeking the Single Thread: the Conceptual Quest in Thompson, P. and Walker, M. (eds) *The Routledge Doctoral Student's Companion: getting to grips with research in education and the social sciences*. London and New York: Routledge

Sunuodula, M and Feng, A (2010) English language education for the linguistic minorities: case of Uyghurs. In A. Feng (ed) *English language in education and society in Greater China*. Bristol: Multilingual Matters

Thaxton, R A (2008) *Catastrophe and contention in rural China: Mao's Great Leap Forward famine and the origins of righteous resistance in Da Fo village*. Cambridge: Cambridge University Press

Townson, D (1999) Cultural Revolution (1966-76). In D. Townson (ed) *A Dictionary of Contemporary History*. Oxford: Blackwell

Wagner, K V (2005) *What is personality*. (Available online) (URL: http://psychology.about.com/od/overviewofpersonality/a/persondef.htm). (Accessed 09 Feb 2008)

Walder, A G (2009) *Fractured Rebellion: The Beijing Red Guard Movement*. Cambridge, Mass. and London: Harvard University Press

Walker, M (2008) Capability formation and education, in B. Lingard, J. Nixon and S. Ranson, S. (eds) *Transforming Learning in Schools and Communities: the remaking of education for a cosmopolitan society.* London and New York: Continuum

Watt, J (1980) Performance of overseas postgraduate students: a management teacher's view. In The British Council (ed) *109-study modes and academic development of overseas students.* London: The British Council, p38-43

Whyte, M K (ed) (2010) *One Country, Two Societies: rural-urban inequality in contemporary China.* Cambridge Mass. and London: Harvard University Press

Williams, C (2003) *Learning in two languages: professional development for bilingual provision in health care education.* Bangor: University of Wales

Williams, M and Burden, R L (2000) *Psychology for language teachers: a social constructive approach.* Beijing: Foreign Language Teaching and Research Press with the syndicate of the Press of the University of Cambridge.

Xinhua (2005) Quiet pink revolution in dark before dawn? *Chinaview*, 26th Dec, 2005 http://news.xinhuanet.com/english/2005-12/26/content_3970520.htm[Accessed 23/06/2010]

Xinhua (2010) National college entrance exam begins with safety. *China Daily*, 7 June http://www.chinadaily.com.cn/china/2010-06/07/content_9945498.htm [Accessed 05/08/2010]

Yang, R (2011a) Chinese ways of thinking in the transformation of China's higher education system, in J. Ryan (ed) *China's Higher Education Reform and Internationalisation.* London and New York: Routledge

Yang, R (2011b) Cultural perspectives on higher education reforms in China since 1978, in B. Adamson, J. Nixon and F. Su (eds) *The Reorientation of Higher Education: compliance and defiance,* Comparative Education Research Centre (CERC), The University of Hong Kong/Springer (forthcoming)

Yang, R and Welch, A R (2010) Globalisation, transnational academic mobility and the Chinese knowledge diaspora: an Australian case study, *Discourse: Studies in the Cultural Politics of Education*, 31 (5), p593-607

Zhou, X (2010) A narrative exploration of the UK academic acculturation experiences of students from mainland China. Unpublished PhD thesis, University of Manchester, UK

Zhou, X (2005) Expectation versus reality: cultural difficulties of Chinese students in the United Kingdom. Unpublished MA dissertation, Peking University, China

Zhou, X (2003) Cultural identification and the second language grammaticality in speech: three cases of Chinese college graduates in the UK. Unpublished paper for the postgraduate module 'Empirical Research Methods in Languages Studies', Peking University, China

Index

153

Chinese Learning Journeys:
Chasing the Dream